# THE E-MYTH

## EVOLUTION

Published by SuccessBooks®, Lake Mary, FL.

SuccessBooks® is a registered trademark.

LCCN: 2024917068
ISBN: 979-8-9892734-8-5

This publication is designed to provide accurate and authoritative information with regard to the subject matter covered. It is sold with the understanding that the publisher is not engaged in rendering legal, accounting, or other professional advice. If legal advice or other expert assistance is required, the services of a competent professional should be sought. The opinions expressed by the authors in this book are not endorsed by SuccessBooks® and are the sole responsibility of the author rendering the opinion.

Most SuccessBooks® titles are available at special quantity discounts for bulk purchases for sales promotions, premiums, fundraising, and educational use. Special versions or book excerpts can also be created to fit specific needs.

For more information, please write:

SuccessBooks®
3415 W. Lake Mary Blvd. #950370
Lake Mary, FL 32746
or call 1.877.261.4930

Visit us online at: www.CelebrityPressPublishing.com.

# THE E-MYTH EVOLUTION

SUCCESS
BOOKS®
Lake Mary, FL

# CONTENTS

# CHAPTER 1

# THE E-MYTH PHENOMENON

By Michael Gerber

**N**o matter how many years have passed since the founding of The E-Myth way back in 1977, since I first created it as The Michael Thomas Corp. with my then good buddy Tom Travisano—may he rest in peace—not much has changed in the reality that prompted our work.

Think of everything that has transpired in the world of business since the '70s and the tens of millions of companies that have started up since then. Yet the failure rate continues to be obscene for small and emerging companies. Indeed, one may be tempted to say that if the problems remain the same after all the work done in the interceding years, have any of us made any difference at all?

But when I parse the data, I don't find businesses are failing because the material in the *E-Myth* books and all the other business books is somehow now archaic. So why is it, then, that the problems persist in the millions of startups year after year after year? The reason I believe we haven't seen much change is that human nature hasn't much changed.

Those who start their outreach to make it on their own have already committed the first fatal flaw. They are going at it on their own! They don't prepare by studying, reading, and listening to others who have a wealth of experience. For some reason, they don't think of starting their own business as something that millions of others have already done. So they go at it impulsively, without a single thought as to why they will most certainly fail, like the many millions who have failed before them.

The motivating factors for the business owners who fail are remarkably similar:

- They do it in the main to get rid of having a boss.

- They're inspired by their proven ability to do the work they have learned how to do so well, thinking that they already know how to do what they're setting out to do, so why in the world would they study how to do it?

- They think they already know how to run a business, as they've spent so many years doing it without anyone's help, so how in the world could they possibly fail?

And so they set out on their own, just like all those fools before them. And they blow it, of course. Just like those before them.

No, businesses aren't failing because guidance was hard to find but because in order for a business owner to succeed, they need to be willing to stand on the shoulders of the giants who came before them. Learn from others' mistakes! Read, study, ask questions, and get prepared.

The good news is that not all start-ups are failing. All is not lost. Quite the opposite, because over the past four decades, some difference *was* made! And is being made.

Monumental differences!

If you don't believe me, you're holding the proof in your very hands. In the following pages you'll read the culmination of just some of the successful ventures entrepreneurs have embarked on— where they began, what they wanted, and the obstacles they ran into along the way.

You'll get a taste of the process entrepreneurs took, starting with knowing what mistakes to avoid and practices to employ, that put them at the head of the pack. These business owners worked hard. They reaped the benefits. They defied the statistics.

These many stories attest to the stunning evolution of The

E-Myth. As for me, I've been in an evolutionary process of my own. For the past decade my wife and partner, Luz Delia Gerber, and I have been artfully, dedicatedly, intensely focused on creating what we think of as The NEW E-Myth here at Michael E. Gerber Companies. This process has challenged us, provoked us, stimulated us, and blessed us with discoveries of our dream, vision, purpose, and mission to degrees far beyond anything we anticipated when we stepped out on this path all those years ago.

What did we find?

We found that the word *new* belies the truth that lies at the very heart of it.

The evolution of The E-Myth wasn't *new* but simply reinforced the provocative genius that resided for all these years at the very heart of it. That is not to say my genius, no. That's to say the true genius, "born in the image of G-d, born to create, born to create a world fit for G-d," was the true genius that inspired my E-Myth work—from the very beginning of it to this very moment now, as you're reading these words.

Indeed, had we pursued the vast network of followers whose lives have been transformed by the work we've done, this book would be filled with tens of thousands of chapters. An infinite medley of stories, on and on and on, touching upon every imaginable and, yes, unimaginably vibrant insight into the countless innovations we've been party to over all these years, with all these stunning participants.

I thank G-d we've been able to touch the many "smallest of the small," for the fact of that and the profound act of that has led us to today, where we're celebrating the evolution of The E-Myth with the stories that follow, and the many that will follow in the countless stories we intend to share with you in the future.

At the age of eighty-eight, I'm proud to read and share these beautiful stories, of leaders I've influenced with my work over the past half century, since the invention of the E-Myth phenomenon. These practices have touched the lives of millions upon millions of small business owners around the world. Yours may be one of the countless many whose stories follow on the heels of those you're about to read.

G-d bless, and will His *wonders* never cease! Blessing you and those you touch. With everything Luz Delia and I have done, and will continue to do, may G-d keep us strong!

## About Michael

Michael E. Gerber is the legend behind the *E-Myth* series of books, including *The E-Myth Revisited*, *E-Myth Mastery*, *The E-Myth Manager*, *The E-Myth Enterprise*, *The Most Successful Small Business in the World*, and *Awakening the Entrepreneur Within*. Collectively, his books have sold millions of copies worldwide.

He is the founder of the new Evolution of the Enterprise: The Hierarchy of Growth. The foundation of this new venture is The Course and The Program, both of which are being introduced to transform one-person companies into one-thousand-person companies, throughout the world, the economic marvel of our time. It's a program that supports entrepreneurs with the creation of turnkey ventures.

He is chairman of the Michael E. Gerber Companies™, a highly sought-after speaker, and a consultant who has trained tens of thousands of business owners and clients, and has millions of readers worldwide. Michael lives with his wife, Luz Delia, in Carlsbad, California.

# CHAPTER 2

# WHEN GOD CALLS, ANSWER!

By Luz Delia Gerber, Mrs. E-Myth

## A NEW BEGINNING

I didn't know anything about Mr. Michael E. Gerber when I received the invitation to his keynote speech. I'd never heard him speak, and I hadn't read his books. I just knew Joe, one of my trusted massage practitioners, swore reading his work would transform my business, rejuvenate Inc.—and my life.

I politely took Joe's copy, which I had no intention of reading. At the time, all I consumed were works on well-being. I had little interest in (or time for) business mindset books. I didn't even consider what I did every day a business!

Joe sensed my lack of enthusiasm.

"Listen, Luz Delia, I won't massage you again until you've read that book," he said. "Seriously. That's how much I believe in it."

Take my weekly massage away?

This was 1996. My reflexology operation was open from 9 a.m. to 9 p.m. seven days a week. Working on people's feet for those long hours was physically demanding, and I would have done anything to keep my standing massage appointment with Joe.

So I solemnly promised to read the book. Once I started, I read it overnight. I couldn't put it down!

In the morning, a client invited me to go listen to a popular speaker. When I turned the postcard around, guess who was there, leaning on his *E-Myth Revisited* book? Mr. Gerber himself! Holy moly! I still have that little card.

Within three days I was sitting in the front row in a large room with 289 other people. From the moment Mr. Gerber took the stage, he commanded the space and audience. I was a sponge, absorbing every detail and nuance. I'd never been so captivated by a message and its delivery.

Michael embodied all the lessons and wisdom in his book, and even sitting in that crowded room, I felt a spotlight on him and me. Hundreds of people were around, yet for me, nobody else was in that room that day. He was speaking only to me!

After his talk I was elated and amazed. I took Joe's book and had Mr. Gerber personalize the copy to him. I then offered to massage him.

"Can you be in my room in an hour," he asked without hesitation, handing me his hotel key.

I rushed to my office and canceled all my appointments. With my massage table in hand, I went to nurture Mr. Gerber.

I knew I had experienced something profound, but I didn't yet know how transformative that day would be. I didn't know I would receive private mentorship from this world-renowned business heart and mind. I didn't know my entire company and business mindset would forever change.

Also, Joe didn't tell me that years later I would become Mrs. E-Myth! Marrying this beautiful soul and sharing a new, unknown, wonderful life together as partners in love and business.

## A LIFE DEDICATED TO HEALING

Growing up, Daddy was a Pentecostal minister, so I've always known God and trusted His presence. Although I didn't often understand (or follow) God's messages, I learned there were consequences or rewards for paying or *not* paying attention to them! Experience quickly taught me that if I asked God a question, I always got an answer. It might not be the answer or time frame I expected, yet I did indeed receive an answer.

I always trusted God would show me the next right step, and He delivered big in October 1985, when I met renowned naturopath, health practitioner, and Mother of Wheatgrass, Dr. Ann

Wigmore. After meeting at her house, we were immediately enamored with each other, and she became my mentor and close friend. I struggled with health issues then, including fibromyalgia, H. pylori, and chronic fatigue syndrome. To start my healing process, I took her advice and began treating food as medicine. She gifted me with this beautiful statement: "Let food be thy medicine and medicine be thy food!"

Soon I was consulting with people on Ann's program, which focused on natural, chemical-free, pesticide-free living foods. The program included seeds, nuts, vegetables, grains sprouted right in her kitchen, Rejuvelac, almond cream, and veggie kraut! I also began putting events together for her. She certified me as a Living Foods Lifestyle Consultant, which quickly segued into my mentorship and well-being business.

I took my clients through a health-focused supermarket chain almost daily, and my constant presence soon caught the attention of the manager, Mark "Flash" Dixon. Upon meeting, it was another instant connection. Enamored with my energy, he offered me the opportunity to set up a small corner in the store to do my reflexology work on store patrons.

The media eventually took up my story, and before I knew it, I was creating corporate well-being days for some of the globe's biggest companies, including Chevron, Intel, Sterling Bank, William M. Mercer, and Administaff. I offered massages, sprouting, and consulting with their cafeterias on better food choices.

Through all this I never felt as if I knew what I was doing. My intentional desire was simply to serve anyone who came through my doors. I knew God was working through my hands, even if I didn't understand what I was doing! I had learned repeatedly that God gives you messages, and if you don't pay attention, that window of opportunity He opened can close. So I remained an ignorant kid playing in a sandbox. I sat on my little wooden bench, played with people's feet, from children to seniors, and continued to educate myself on the wondrous workings and interconnectivity of human anatomy. Having always had a passion for the human body and all God's elements and creatures, I eventually went to massage school and other modalities and was certified.

After a few years my little corner had expanded into an eight-hundred-square-foot space with twelve chairs and twenty-three massage practitioners. I found myself a business owner and manager who had pulled in hundreds of thousands in income in just my first six months.

This was when Michael entered my life.

After watching his speech and offering my massage work as thanks, Michael made a generous, unexpected offer to mentor me. No way was I passing up this opportunity God had just presented!

For about a year, as our schedules allowed, we texted, called, and met up when he visited Houston to keynote. He repeatedly talked about not being a technician and pushing my vision beyond being a manager. My last homework assignment was to find my replacement for my reflexology business and to take up my leadership training with him, which he was offering as a gift!

When we next met for dinner at a beautiful restaurant, he immediately asked whether I'd found my replacement.

"Oh," I said, a bit taken aback. "I can't *actually* do that."

I ran my own practice and pulled in half a million a year. I figured something was working. But Michael was serious and insistent.

"Are you committed to creating a global entity with your business or not? You have a beautiful vision, but it will go away unless you begin anew!"

I had no clue what he was talking about. When I wouldn't commit, Michael stood, handed me his business card, and said, "When you're ready to get serious about your vision and business, call me."

Then he walked out of the restaurant, leaving me alone at the table. Embarrassed and flustered, I sat for a while before getting up and leaving myself. What an *asshole*!

During our mentorship Michael always said business owners

who insisted on being technicians had ten years. Maximum. They'd struggle and stress and then quit or close.

"You're going to kill this beautiful dream of yours," he'd say. "Or it's going to kill you."

When Michael left that restaurant, I was eight years into my business. Two years later—almost ten years to the date of starting my little company—I passed out from a neglected systemic tooth infection and almost died. It took years to recover.

I ended up moving to New Mexico to spend time healing and reevaluating my life. One day, after noticing I felt better, I was working through a difficult issue, and God sent me another message.

"Call Michael."

I immediately did, and he answered. This was in 2003.

Soon after reentering each other's lives, Michael confessed his love. He recalled every detail from the day we met. My royal blue dress with the buttons. The way I had worn my hair. It turns out he had also felt we were the only two people in the room that day.

We married on my birthday, March 4, 2006.

From the moment I met Michael, I knew he was special, and being with someone like that was often overwhelming. As I always do in uncertain times, I asked God for guidance.

"How do I navigate being with someone who's larger than life?"

The answer came effortlessly. God had gifted me this man, visionary, and amazing soul. He'd also gifted me the wisdom and strength to walk beside him, forging my path while inspiring him and allowing him to walk his own road.

## BUILDING YOUR LEGACY

The greatest wisdom I've taken from Michael's teachings is your business must never trap you. It's created to free you. Stir your imagination. Appreciate and honor the moment, energy, time, and space for what you love. Inspire and guide you. Highlight and elevate what you're best at. It's meant to align deeply with the mark you desire and intend to leave on this planet.

## Dream! Vision! Purpose! Mission!

Whatever path you choose, awaken your dream, vision, purpose, and mission. With complete clarity on those four masterpieces, you're on a path to sustaining, rewarding, important work.

Michael and I first launched the Dreaming Room™ in 2005. For this, Amethyst, my youngest daughter, and I embarked on the exciting new venture of producing a "show." It was stunning! I immediately saw a profound change in how Michael approached his students. When he spoke to audiences of ten thousand plus, he'd be the first to admit he routinely yelled *at* them. (Sometimes foul language was even used.) He believed passionately in his message about freeing people from the trap of "working only *in*" their businesses.

When he started the Dreaming Room™, that approach stopped. He wasn't yelling at people anymore. He engaged and asked questions. The shift was intimate and beautiful to watch. The questions were still pointed and poignant, yet he asked compassionately. To awaken the dreamer within, you must begin with your dream, and he was unveiling a dreamer's inherent power. He was showing people how getting clarity and leading with a dream awakens and inspires ordinary people to do extraordinary things. How, when you understand the heart behind the company, you accomplish possibilities you never thought of!

For true success in your life and business, ask questions that dig deeper than money. Find meaning and what provokes you to work with focus and intentionality. When business owners go through that exercise, they start the transformational journey from technician to entrepreneur.

## Be prepared for divine change.

Nothing in business stays the same forever. As you and your business evolve, expect to revisit your dream, vision, purpose, and mission. Keep tweaking its energy to align with your current intentions without vacillation! Once you clearly see your dream, march forth until you reach your first benchmark. Then the next. Tweak and continue. You're almost there! Be hot or cold rather than warm!

With clarity in your current moment, you're ready for the next action. To turn that job into a practice. To transform your practice into a business. And once you're ready, that business can become an enterprise haven. Think McDonald's. It's the world's most successful and continually growing small business!

You can do this work yourself—use the example manifesto on our website as a starting point, or get full mentorship by participating in the Dreaming Room™. However you get there, that clarity positions you for victory and makes room for what's important in your life, including your family and the people you serve!

Many go into business thinking they're creating opportunities for their loved ones. Then they get so stuck in the cycle of keeping that business afloat that they end up with even *less* time to dedicate to what truly matters.

Once you discover your dream, vision, purpose, and mission, you're ready to create and document processes and systems that allow your company to achieve those ideals without your constant involvement. That's magical! That's when you're in a position to leave financial stability for your family and build a legacy that serves generations to come, all while having the freedom, energy, and time to devote to the important things! You can do that!

And you don't have to know how to do it all now. Your first step is *awakening the entrepreneur within*—the one you were born with!

## MY DREAM FOR THE FUTURE

My dream is to create a more fulfilling, more secure future for women and children. As a mother to three brilliant daughters, a grandmother to five beautiful granddaughters and one brilliant, handsome grandson, and a great-grandmother to a wonderful great-grandson, I'm keenly aware our children and the feminine woman are our future. That's why I proudly support charitable children endeavors and the Our Children~~THEIR Future Foundation™.

As the stewards of these amazing kids, our work is opening the windows in this lifetime and letting them see the sunlight. Showing them how unique and brilliant they each are. Allowing them to feel how each one is an incredible, limitless beam of light. Encouraging them to seize opportunities and to realize all options are available to them.

I see a future where the elderly are welcomed into the family dynamic and community. So much wisdom, love, and nurturing can be shared between our babies and our elderly, and everyone benefits from that togetherness.

I wish to empower strong, independent women, dispelling this harmful idea that being a self-sufficient woman in any way threatens her relationship with her partner. There's nothing better for our collective future than independent, self-sufficient married women. An independent, happily married woman inspiring herself and her spouse in their endeavors and bearing the children God grants is a beautiful thing!

My big dream is the manifestation of a foundation and community that foster this culture. Working with young mothers and their children thrills me and fills me with energy, joy, and purpose. I imagine the great honor of creating a safe place that inspires women to speak and be heard and that generates good, love, and light for generations.

Yes, that dream is ambitious, yet I've had decades working beside Michael and watching people use his teachings to make big dreams come true. So I know mine is possible, and I know it's possible for anyone else out there discovering and inventing the extraordinary!

Are you ready?

## About Luz

Luz Delia Gerber's journey into entrepreneurship and personal growth began unexpectedly with a demand from her massage therapist to read *The E-Myth Revisited*. Little did she know, this pivotal moment would redefine her path. From 1988 to 2003, she thrived at rejuvenate®, her small business inside Whole Foods Market managed by Mark Dixon. Along the way, she encountered Michael E. Gerber, author of the book that started it all, leading to a love story that culminated in marriage in 2006.

Today, Luz Delia embraces a multifaceted role. She supports her husband's vision as his business partner by day and explores her creative side during early mornings and evenings. An avid meditator, she finds inspiration in nature, especially by water, and cherishes moments of sunrise and sunset as opportunities for spiritual connection.

Family is paramount for Luz Delia. She takes joy in her daughters and grandchildren, who enrich her life with their presence. Beyond family, her passion extends to her aspiration to serve others, particularly through their nonprofit foundation, Our Children~~THEIR Future.Foundation™, launching this year. This endeavor aims to empower children, young girls, and women across generations, reflecting her commitment to nurturing the feminine spirit.

Reflecting on her journey, Luz Delia finds fulfillment in personal growth and well-being. Inspired by mentors like Dr. Ann Wigmore, she advocates for holistic living and shares her insights on well-being through writings and teachings. Her ultimate goal is to foster a new paradigm of well-being for future generations.

Luz Delia's dedication to serving others is rooted in a newfound understanding: to serve others completely, she must first serve herself. This philosophy drives her to share her journey of self-discovery and well-being with others, advocating for love, joy, and fulfillment in every aspect of life.

As she continues to co-create with Michael E. Gerber through their company, she remains committed to empowering small business owners worldwide. Their collaborative efforts aim not only to help entrepreneurs succeed but to find joy and purpose in their endeavors, transforming lives along the way.

Luz Delia Gerber's life is a testament to the transformative power of embracing one's personal journey and sharing the lessons learned with others. Her story is one of love, growth, and a profound commitment to making a meaningful difference in the world.

# CHAPTER 3

# ROAD TRIPS AND REVELATIONS

*How One Book Changed My Life*

By Gordon Bruner

"Wait," I said, trying to wrap my head around the conversation. "How much money is left, exactly?"

"Enough to last us two more days."

The words hit me like a gut punch. I couldn't understand. We had people whose job it was to ensure this kind of thing never happened. I had employees depending on me. Now the entire company was on the brink. What had gone wrong?

I allowed myself to be stunned and upset for a few minutes. Then I accepted reality and started making calls. I left for a week, visiting customer after customer of my facilities construction and maintenance company.

When I returned, I had a million dollars in checks. Some of those funds were for money owed. Some customers paid for projects that hadn't even started yet.

I was only able to pull that rabbit out of the hat because I had built a company on the foundation of trust, belief, and honesty. My customers knew without a doubt that they could pay me in advance and the job would still be done. Because I had been there for them, they were willing to be there for me.

No one is saying scaling a company is easy. No one is saying it's not without its challenges and growing pains. But with integrity and a willingness to adjust, learn, and grow, any problem is surmountable and any goal is achievable.

## THE PURCHASE THAT CHANGED EVERYTHING

At sixteen, I took a job at a supermarket. I worked at that same supermarket until I was twenty-eight. Eventually following my entrepreneurial calling, I cashed out my retirement and started a pizza business with a friend. We bought one to start and ended up with four total. I didn't think about it at the time, but this was my first attempt at scaling and growing a business. Unfortunately, we soon ran into the bumps of business ownership. I realized we had a cancer in the building that couldn't be removed, so one Friday night I fired everyone. (This was not a good decision!) I brought in my mom, partner, and neighbors. Anyone who would listen to me and help me make pizzas. We started over by hiring all new people, and I sold out after nine years.

I then ended up in the vending business, working my way from one soft drink machine to sixty. Through connections made in my vending machine business, I landed in maintenance work and ended up founding the Volunteer Maintenance Co. in 1998.

Before I knew it, I was bouncing all over the country fixing broken things. For ten years I lived out of a suitcase, traveling constantly for that business. Because I spent so much time behind the wheel, I started listening to books on tape. (This was long before digital streaming!)

In 2000 I went to the self-help section at a local bookstore in search of my latest purchase. There, I first saw Michael Gerber's *The E-Myth*. I'd read many business development books, but this one's description stood out.

I immediately realized this wasn't just an examination of why to run a business or what others had done to launch their businesses. This was designed to teach you how to run a business. It was a nuts-and-bolts step-by-step blueprint for success. Every piece was broken down to the smallest denominator.

As I listened to the story of Mary the baker, I felt echoes of my own story. Mary was amazing at making pies. (She was a great pie-making technician.) So, she set out to run her own pie-making business. But just because Mary was great at making pies, it didn't mean she would be great at running a business.

At that point in my career I was Mary. I was a great technician, but I hadn't put any processes or systems in place to create a business that could operate without my direct, constant involvement. Without me, there was no business. The book laid out how to break free of that cycle.

Listening to *The E-Myth* was a profound experience. Everything made so much sense, and I fell in love with the simple but actionable plan to transition from technician to entrepreneur. Within one year of listening to that book, I bought and moved into a five-thousand-square-foot office space. I started bringing in people. I shifted my role from doing all the boots-on-the-ground work to being more of a manager.

From that operation of one out of my beaten-up truck, I started the journey that eventually turned into VMC Facilities, a construction and maintenance company licensed and bonded to do business in eleven states and registered to do business in another eleven.

## GOODBYE, TECHNICIAN. HELLO, ENTREPRENEUR.

From a guy with $1,500 in his pocket and a rusty pickup, I've grown a highly successful multimillion-dollar business. Looking back, the journey seems amazing, but I did it all on the back of some simple philosophies.

### Pounce.

I never want to pass up an opportunity that comes my way. I'd rather pounce now than regret it later. The main difference between a successful and unsuccessful person? One sits around talking about doing something. The other goes out and does it.

When you see a chance, pounce.

### Stop being the technician.

You can only make so much money with two hands, but think what you can accomplish by managing hundreds of hands.

My biggest takeaway from Gerber's work was I needed to stop being the technician in my business. After years of doing the work myself, stepping away felt a bit like putting my kid on the school bus for the first time, but I realized growth was only possible when I implemented processes, procedures, and policies that allowed others to be technicians within this bigger system we were building.

My job was to be out front leading, not standing behind and pushing. I had to find ways to motivate and inspire the people under me. That role would allow me to grow a scalable business.

### Life gets in the way...if you let it.

No matter how many books you read or structures you develop, life tries to get in the way. People. Jobs. Customer problems. In the chaos of day-to-day reality, it's easy to start putting out fires and lose focus.

This is especially true because every business needs people, and once people start interacting, you have challenges, problems, emotions, needs, and unpredictability. In those moments, you must be a business owner, but you also must be willing to be a human.

In this balancing act, you can't let yourself get distracted from the goal. You've got to fight every inch of the way to keep clarity and focus.

### Revisit everything.

I believe in my heart growth only happens when you keep feeding your brain positive information. Go buy books. Find those nuggets of inspiration and wisdom. You might read an entire book and only take away an impactful sentence or two. It's still worth the effort.

Go back to past material, and revisit what you've learned. Remind yourself of those powerful lessons. Sometimes it's not that you don't know something. It's just that you forgot. Relistening to what motivated you before refreshes your spirit and reenergizes you.

And don't forget processes must be revisited too. As your company grows, you'll find that what worked yesterday won't work tomorrow. Everything is always evolving, and if processes and policies don't adjust to that evolution, they'll stop being effective.

To be a well-oiled machine that grows sustainably, instill these ideas in your people too. Make education a company priority.

Becoming successful doesn't happen instantly. You have to learn things. Then practice. Then relearn them. Then go back all over again as you grow and change over time.

## Make policies and procedures around growth.

Successful, growing companies need guidelines. You can't get by on faith alone. Prioritize your company's growth, and then put someone in charge of that process. (As a disciplined ex-military guy, my brother was a natural choice for my company.)

As you scale and get busier, it's easy to push those growth meetings off to next week. Then the next. Then they never happen.

Create a clear segregation of duties to ensure everyone can succeed in their role. Have checks and balances to safeguard against problems and keep everyone accountable.

After we implemented our five-year growth plan, I got to a point where I didn't go into the office for months. I could just stay away and let everyone do their job.

I went to Texas once for a five-day trip, and it turned into ten months. The business kept running smoothly. That's the power of creating, documenting, and implementing organizational policies, procedures, and systems.

## Do the right thing for the right reasons.

It's so much easier to take care of existing customers than to hunt down new clients. How do you keep those customers? By always doing the right thing. People do business with people they know and trust. When you do your job to the best of your ability, give people that level of trust, and pay attention to the details, customers reward you with their loyalty.

In my business I'm not selling someone a pair of shoes. I need them to trust me with their multimillion-dollar construction projects, so the presence of integrity and honesty is all the more important.

Success happens when two things come together: actions and intentions. You must do the right things, but it also has to be for the right reasons. I've never done anything just for the money. I did it because I liked it. I wanted to do a good job and be there for my customers. Sure, you have to make money to run a business. But if you do it strictly for the cash, you lose something essential, and you'll always find success just escapes you.

## Attitude matters.

I once had a malignant melanoma. After surgery I denied all treatment. My scans showed I was cancer-free, and every scan for five years after showed the same thing. My doctor told me my attitude throughout that time was one reason I had a successful outcome.

Your attitude matters. It has real, tangible effects. Everyone has personal struggles, but you can overcome any challenge. It's all in your heart and head. You just have to want an outcome more than you're afraid of it.

I was walking through the American Civil War Museum in Richmond, Virginia, when I came across a flag that read "Any fate but submission." That's life. The successful person knows circumstances might get you, but it's not because you didn't try.

Once I let go of fear and pushed for better, an amazing opportunity-filled life opened up. When you stop wishing for the best and start trying for the best, success follows.

## Build with the end in mind.

As you grow your business, start with the end goal in mind. How are you going to step out of your technician role? What's your exit strategy? Work backward from those eventual goals to build your road map. Without that you can't hope to know where you're going.

## Consistency is key.

When we first started implementing policies and procedures, it was overwhelming. So we turned to other companies. We looked at what they were doing, and we adopted and amended the ones we liked.

The biggest theme to emerge was consistency. From how you onboard to when you distribute paychecks to how you make bank deposits, your aim should be consistency. This makes every process clear, easy, and repeatable—even if you experience churn and lose an employee.

Consistency also means everyone knows you're dependable. Whether I've been paid or not, my subcontractors know I'll pay net thirty. Every time. My employees know when to expect their paychecks. Every time.

Following through on what you say is how you build trust, and trust is the capital that keeps your business alive.

## Have the hard conversation (in person or over the phone).

Don't avoid the hard stuff. Get it over with quickly because the more you think about it, the more you build it up in your mind. Have that hard, uncomfortable conversation. Nine times out of ten it's not as bad as you think.

So many today hide behind emails or texts, but there's no emotion there. If you need to solve a problem or get to the bottom of something, pick up the phone and call. You can usually resolve a lingering issue in five minutes with a real conversation.

The worst thing you can do is leave someone hanging. Give people an answer, even if that answer is that you don't know but will find out.

## Build policies and procedures for your life.

Achieving true success isn't just about the business side. You also need success in your personal life. Using the same principles of creating policies and procedures, you can build a structure within your life to accomplish personal goals. (Making time for your passions, as the years pass quickly. Being present for your family and friends, as those are the deepest, most meaningful relationships.)

Sometimes it's simply being brutally honest about who you need out of your life—those who bring nothing but drama and grief. These are people with no real interest in fixing their problems, and if you let them, they can knock you off course.

It's liberating to learn how to never get defeated. To never let anyone hurt your feelings. To only spend time with people you want to be with, not people you need. To be happy being alone sometimes.

Life is full of personal challenges, and success isn't a straight line to the top. It's a series of ups and downs, but once you make up your mind to succeed, life becomes much easier.

## THE LEARNING'S NEVER DONE

I've been running VMC Facilities now for twenty-six years. I was forty when I started, and it's been an absolute whirlwind. Throughout the journey, even when we were two days away from financial ruin, my guiding principle has always been to do the right thing, no matter how painful. That builds unbelievable trust with your customers, and when you have that—plus strategic growth-minded policies and procedures—anything is possible.

In all the books I've read and programs I've gone through, I've never seen a framework for success done better than in *The E-Myth*. It's an easy-to-understand step-by-step code for how to scale and grow. It completely changed how I think about business, and it set my life on a path that's more fulfilling, rewarding, and free than I ever could have imagined.

Because this book enabled me to grow, I've been able to build a business that sustains so many others. I've been able to show up every day doing what I do best, and as I continue to learn from these lessons, I know I'm building my legacy around me every day.

## About Gordon

Gordon Bruner, born as the second child in a family of five, experienced a humble yet enriching childhood in Michigan. Despite financial constraints, Gordon's upbringing was filled with love and taught him the value of resourcefulness. Growing up, he quickly learned the importance of adaptability and acquiring new skills to navigate through life's challenges.

Relocating to Halls Crossroads, a suburb of Knoxville, Tennessee, during his second-grade years, Gordon's journey into the workforce commenced at the age of sixteen with a job at Winn-Dixie, a local grocery store. Realizing that traditional schooling wasn't aligning with his aspirations, he opted to earn his GED and focused on carving his path in the working world.

Ascending the ranks to become a store manager by the age of twenty-eight, Gordon's entrepreneurial spirit ignited as he ventured into various business endeavors, including a Little Caesars franchise and a vending machine company. Despite achieving success, he felt something crucial was absent—a deeper sense of purpose.

The turning point came when Gordon crossed paths with Larry Hayne, a customer whose relentless persistence taught him the value of tenacity. This encounter led to the birth of VMC Facilities LLC in January 1998, marking a significant shift toward a career that resonated with his passions.

Embracing challenges in service-oriented roles, Gordon found joy in problem-solving and embarked on a quest to secure contracts with renowned establishments such as Ruby Tuesday and Chili's restaurants. Through unwavering determination and a relentless pursuit of opportunities, he expanded VMC Facilities LLC's footprint across thirty-three states.

Inspired by the ethos encapsulated in the battle flag motto, "Any fate but submission," Gordon adopted a philosophy of resilience, vowing never to surrender in the face of adversity. Despite encountering economic fluctuations and setbacks, he remained steadfast in his resolve, refusing to succumb to defeat.

Driven by an unwavering determination to overcome obstacles, Gordon Bruner exemplifies the spirit of resilience and perseverance. With his mantra of "Any fate but submission," he continues to forge ahead, undeterred by challenges, and steadfastly pursuing his vision of success.

# CHAPTER 4

# ACHIEVING MORE BY DOING LESS

*How to Have the Best Conversation in the Room*

By Nick Nanton

A s a young, eager songwriter in the competitive music business, I once found myself writing with a musician about forty years older than me. He invited me to write and collaborate with a handful of other musicians, but my invitation came with a stipulation.

"Don't come into that room thinking you have the only idea. Everyone there has written two songs a day for thirty years. They have lots of number ones under their belts," he said. "I'm inviting you because you're talented, and I want you to bring your ideas. But let's also assume you have a lot to learn from everyone else in the room."

From that amazing invitation, I learned a valuable lesson. The best song you can write is the best song in the room that day, and that song comes about through the collaboration of everyone involved. Done the right way, that song couldn't have been written any other way. When everyone brings together their unique skills, perspectives, and talents, it creates an end product that's more dynamic, impactful, and nuanced than anything a single creator could make alone.

This was a powerful lesson early on in my career about how to create a successful project. Identify the unique value I bring. Focus on those areas of innate strength. Collaborate with others, and trust in their innate strengths. Just as Michael Gerber outlines in *The E-Myth*, you can try to do it all yourself, but that path leads to burnout, a lack of fulfillment, and that constant feeling that there aren't ever enough hours in the day.

By the time I started making documentaries, I knew one of my greatest abilities was being able to show up and think on my feet. For my first two documentary projects, I leaned heavily into that ability. I arrived at each shooting location and joyfully declared, "Let's make a documentary."

Eventually I realized that wasn't the best way to operate. I needed to be more grounded in research and legwork. But there was a problem. I don't like research. I've never been the person who thrives by reading and watching material ahead of time.

Luckily, I recognized where I had a deficit and brought on a story producer. Her unique ability is devouring information and simplifying it into the best form for different purposes (podcast outlines, documentary outlines).

Just as it took all those songwriters combining their unique talents to create the best song in the room, I brought that collaborative spirit to my filmmaking. I got to outsource a piece of the process I didn't enjoy, and because of that my story producer got to exercise her unique ability. Then her work prepared and allowed me to bring my unique talents to the project.

With everyone playing a role in the process, I became empowered and prepared to make the most of my skills. I had the foundation of preparation but the freedom and leeway to think on my feet, be creative, and engage with people.

I could focus my effort on the thing that comes most naturally to me and brings me the most personal and professional fulfillment: having the best conversation in the room that day.

# FINDING MY WAY TO THE BEST CONVERSATION

While it's never possible to truly reach the mountaintop—there's always another goal—I have had the good fortune of building a fulfilling career that affords me time, energy, and freedom. I get to spend my hours doing what I'm best at while creating projects that put good into the world.

None of this happened overnight, but a few guiding principles and a lot of great mentors helped me along the way.

### Aim to retire early.

Many people dream of the day they can finally retire, but why is that? Because they get to leave behind all the aspects of working that they don't enjoy. They're free to do with their time what they want. Pursue passions. Explore what makes them happy and fulfilled.

But what if you were able to start that process now? What if you could systematically remove the things in your personal and professional life that you didn't love? What if you could free up the mental space, physical space, and energy to dig into what does bring you joy? How would that change your life?

That's the kind of freedom Michael's work hopes to bring to people. When you do every last detail and task in your business, including the ones that aren't in your wheelhouse and bring you no joy, you set yourself on a path toward burnout.

When you adjust your mindset and adopt some of the core principles within *The E-Myth*, you're able to retire—not from work itself but from work that's draining, unfulfilling, and not in your zone of genius.

### Utilize your unique gifts for the benefit of the world.

In order to do the kind of work you like best and leave behind everything else, you first have to identify what strengths and preferences you should be pursuing. This comes down to two factors: what you like the most and what provides the most value to others. When you find an area where those two overlap, you'll know you're onto your unique gifts.

Too often when people start businesses, they try to do everything. They take on the entire logistical and mental burden of running that operation. But you're not uniquely suited to do every task required in a business. Nobody is.

Instead of taking on every responsibility in your business, start with the easy stuff. Focus your attention on those things that come effortlessly and naturally to you. When you identify those skills, you're primed to provide real value to the world doing something you absolutely love.

By utilizing your gifts for the benefit of the world, you break free from the trap of doing work you shouldn't be doing. You unlock the ability to accomplish and to achieve more by doing less.

## Make your gift transferable (and valuable) to the world.

Once you've gone through the exercise of identifying your unique skills and gifts, then it's about translating that knowledge into a transferable skill.

Lots of people have immense talent but never figure out how to direct that into something that provides value to themselves and others.

Take someone like Chris Voss. He had a twenty-four-year career in the FBI, after which he taught at Harvard and Georgetown. He painstakingly took 250 case studies from his time as a high-stakes negotiator and distilled those lessons down into a book. He took his unique gifts, experiences, and perspective and figured out how that could help those around him.

For Chris, his transferable skill was his ability to serve as a teacher and mentor. For me, I have meaningful conversations that lead to produced outcomes.

I have these conversations in front of the camera for podcasts and my shows, including *In Case You Didn't Know*. I also have them behind the camera while making my documentaries or running my business. The vast majority of my day now is spent having these deep, meaningful conversations that end up translating into impactful stories that many can benefit from.

Do I still need to write and respond to emails? Sure. But I've built my business and mindset intentionally to ensure I get to spend the majority of my time doing the things I should be doing.

## Be disciplined and consistent.

Identifying your unique value. Figuring out how to translate that into something that benefits others. Adhering to the boundaries you establish about where you should be investing your time and energy. None of this is easy, and none of it happens overnight.

Stopping yourself from falling into established habits takes discipline. Getting out of your own way and opening yourself to change and growth takes discipline.

It's understandable for that process to feel overwhelming, so start with something concrete and small. Sit down and make a list. Write out all the things you want to get rid of in your life or business this quarter, and then start figuring out how to remove each one. For many, it will require creating and documenting the processes necessary to have others take on those responsibilities. After all, you don't have to (and shouldn't) do everything, but that doesn't mean everything doesn't still have to be done.

If growth and betterment are your aim, you have to be in it for the long haul. Not everything will happen in thirty days—or even a year. It's about constantly and intentionally getting incrementally better.

Eventually the process will feel a bit like remodeling a kitchen. You start with the thing that's causing you the most friction. Those old cabinets. Then, once you replace those, you'll notice the backsplash looks dated. Once that's fixed, you'll want to replace the flooring.

You might never get to a point—in your kitchen, business, or life—where it's 100 percent perfect. But if you keep moving toward what brings you joy and fulfillment and leaving behind what drains you, you will eventually realize you wake up every day motivated to keep going.

## Everyone has their unique talents.

Somewhere out there, there are people who wake up and can't wait to create balance sheets. You might not be that person, but just because you don't enjoy a task doesn't mean it isn't somebody else's passion and talent.

When we operate as if others have the same propensities as us, we're usually bringing a lot of baggage into those assumptions. When you can change your thinking around this, you're better able to let go of that compulsion to personally do every task in your business. You're in the right mindset to create processes that set up others to have more success doing what they love. That, in turn, frees your physical, mental, and emotional energy to focus where you shine.

## Don't take your gifts for granted.

When something comes naturally to you, it's easy to assume two things. One, everyone has that same innate ability and doesn't have to work hard to excel at it. Two, because that talent or ability is something you were born with, it doesn't have incredible power and value. Both are false premises.

The areas where you're naturally gifted are your greatest assets. Don't run away from, belittle, or dismiss the incredible gifts you've been given. Never take them for granted. When you embrace your gifts and build your work and life around them, you put yourself in a position to thrive.

With the entrepreneurial framing laid out in *The E-Myth*, you can build a system where you do more of the things you enjoy and less of the things you don't—all while experiencing more growth, success, and freedom than you imagined possible.

And don't forget, once you build this system, it's OK to feel the pull of impostor syndrome. It's natural to wonder where you and your gifts fit into the world and whether others will be interested in them. (If you don't feel that way at least some of the time, it might be time to push your boundaries and horizons!)

When those thoughts and doubts appear, the important thing is to keep progressing. Keep refining your processes and systems.

Keep pursuing the talents and endeavors that are your natural gifts and that you know will bring tremendous value to others.

## Success always requires hard work.

"Hard work beats talent when talent doesn't work hard."
—High school basketball coach Tim Notke

The important caveat with natural talent is that you still have to work hard to refine those gifts and to figure out how you can best serve the world with those talents. Just because something comes easily doesn't mean you won't have to work hard to see success.

Yes, your talent alone might provide some value to others, but when you put in the work to hone those skills and to think deeply about how you can serve the world, that's when your impact starts to become exponential.

You were given amazing talents. No matter how narrow the scope, you were gifted with the ability to improve the lives of others. A spot was provided for you in this world, and your innate gifts are the best and most natural place to start. Then it's just about focusing your efforts and maximizing your impact.

## Win the best invitations.

When you do niche down deeply into your unique ability, it becomes obvious to those around you how gifted you are in that field. People will want you around because they'll recognize a simple truth. When you insert your unique ability into their lives or businesses, they will grow and improve and have more success because you're there.

What does that mean? When you recognize, own, and refine your zone of genius, you start getting all the best invitations. Better, more interesting, more lucrative opportunities start coming your way because talent attracts talent. Other successful, motivated, purpose-driven individuals will recognize that drive in you and will want to be in your orbit.

# GOING BACK TO THE BEGINNING

In my varied career as a director, producer, songwriter, author, and executive, I have always lived the core tenets within *The E-Myth*. I've always strived to recognize what pursuits bring me fulfillment and joy, and over time I've increasingly orchestrated my working life to focus on those areas with even more purpose and drive.

It's no surprise then that Michael Gerber was the first person ever to receive a lifetime achievement award from our annual SuccessSummit® event. Michael was there at the very beginning, supporting my crazy dream. He believed in me and my quest to translate my unique ability into something special and beneficial to the world.

Fourteen years later we've now honored everyone from Chris Voss to Lisa Nichols. But it started in that fledgling year with Michael, and I'll always be grateful that he acknowledged my innate gifts and played his role in allowing me to continue growing in them.

## About Nick

From the slums of Port-au-Prince, Haiti, with special forces raiding a sex trafficking ring and freeing children, to the Virgin Galactic Space Port in Mojave with Sir Richard Branson, twenty-two-time Emmy Award–winning Director-Producer Nick Nanton has become known for telling stories that connect. Why? Because he focuses on the most fascinating subject in the world: *people*. As an award-winning songwriter, storyteller, and best-selling author, Nick has shared his message with millions of people through his documentaries, speeches, blogs, lectures, songs, and best-selling books. Nick's book *StorySelling* hit The Wall Street Journal Best-Seller List and is available on Audible as an audiobook. Nick has directed more than sixty documentaries and a sold-out Broadway Show (garnering forty-three Emmy nominations in multiple regions and twenty-two wins), including:

- *DICKIE V* (ESPN/Disney+)
- *Rudy Ruettiger: The Walk On* (Amazon Prime)
- *The Rebound* (Netflix)
- *Operation Toussaint* (Amazon Prime)

Nick has shared the stage with, coauthored books with, and made films featuring:

- Larry King
- Kathie Lee Gifford
- Hoda Kotb
- Dick Vitale
- Kenny Chesney
- Magic Johnson
- Coach Mike Krzyzewski
- Jack Nicklaus
- Tony Robbins
- Lisa Nichols
- Peter Diamandis
- And many more

Nick specializes in bringing the element of human connection to every viewer, no matter the subject. He is currently directing and hosting the series *In Case You Didn't Know* (season 1 executive produced by Larry King), featuring legends in the worlds of business, entrepreneurship, personal development, technology, and sports.

Nick's first love has always been music. He has been writing songs for more than two decades, and his songs have been aired on radio across the United States and in Canada. He is currently ranked in the top 10 percent of songwriters in the world. His songs have been recorded by Lee Brice, Darius Rucker, RaeLynn, Joe Bryson, and many more, and have amassed more than three million streams on Spotify, Apple Music, Pandora, and SoundCloud. He received three Gold records in 2018 for his work with the global touring band A Day to Remember.

Nick has written and/or produced songs that have appeared on the following shows or in promotional commercials for:

- the Fox prime-time series *Glee*, *New Girl*, *House*, and *Hell's Kitchen*
- the MLB All-Star Game
- ABC Family's hit series *Falcon Beach*
- the CBS prime-time series *Ghost Whisperer* starring Jennifer Love Hewitt

# CHAPTER 5

# THE CNS WAY

By Bill Dunn

**"Y**ou're doing what?"

I walked into the office of my boss and good friend, taking some deep breaths and trying not to think about the gravity of what I'm about to say to him. This man hired me years ago and mentored me, and I had to tell him I was walking away.

"You're not going to believe this, but at the same time, I hope you're happy for me."

Nobody does what I was doing, not at age fifty, ten years shy of retirement.

"I'm leaving. Not to go work for a competitor. I bought a company."

His facial expression was still set on, *You did what*? "What kind of company?"

In his thirty years in business, managing this large corporation, he had never had anyone in a senior-management level leave the company to start their own business.

"It is a cleaning company. I got a ten-year business loan, and my goal is to pay it off in five."

Then I watched as the shock began to wear off him. He laughed good-naturedly. "I'd be surprised if you didn't do it in four."

———— ◆ ————

It meant a lot to hear that because I knew him to be a great businessperson. It was thanks to Michael Gerber's book *The E-Myth*

*Revisited* that I finally found the confidence I needed. Before the day I offered my resignation, I'd read the book ten times. Always in the back of mind I knew I wouldn't fail if I found the courage to take the leap from working for someone to buying a business.

I also had the benefit of seeing two of my friends who'd also followed Michael's E-Myth system to a tee and had tremendous success. The information in the book was transformational for their businesses, and they both still follow the concepts today.

If you're tired of going to work every day and making someone else all the money, I hope sharing my story will inspire you to believe you can be a successful business owner.

## GOLDEN HANDCUFFS

I worked for most of my career in the wine and spirits business for some major corporations. Then toward the back half of my career, I went to work for one of my customers, a distributor of wholesale alcohol beverages in New Jersey. Always in the back of my mind I wanted to own my own business. My parents are entrepreneurs; my brother's an entrepreneur; my closest friends are entrepreneurs.

The problem was that I'd been so successful in my corporate job, I was making too much money to walk away. I had a great salary, benefits, a fully stocked 401(k). If I stayed, I had the prospect of a higher-level job to look forward to in the years to come. I also still had a mortgage and two kids under ten. I'd grown comfortable in our lifestyle. How could I leave all that?

I also knew if I didn't do this by the time I turned fifty, I wouldn't ever do it. So when I was forty-eight, I buckled down. If I was going to make this happen, I needed to be prepared. I read *E-Myth* again, listened to the audio, read some of Michael's other books, as well as some other business books.

To really take this idea seriously, I would need to pay myself close to my current salary. We couldn't maintain our lifestyle for less. The only way to make that happen was to take out a two-million-dollar loan to buy the company, put a second lien on our home, and use the entirety of my retirement funds. I was throwing all the chips on the table. If it failed, I was a goner. Sure, I could go back to work again, but I'd have no retirement fund and potentially lose my house and have to file for bankruptcy if I didn't pay back the SBA loan.

Everybody, including my father and my friends who had their own businesses, told me, "Don't do it. You've got ten more years left until you retire. You're crazy." And I'd just reply, "I've got to."

If I didn't try, I would be so disappointed in myself. Ten years down the road, when I retired, I would feel as if I'd failed myself. I knew I could do more in my career than just work for somebody else. I also wanted to set a good example for my kids because they saw how unhappy I was going to work for somebody else every day. I had an hour-and-a-half commute each way. That took time away from the family. I'd watched my own dad leave his career in his late forties, and he'd been successful. I was convinced this was the right move, so I began looking in earnest for a business to buy.

# DUE DILIGENCE

I'd already decided I wanted to purchase something in the service industry, a business category I understood. A business that would pose a technical challenge held no interest to me. No roof contracting or HVAC companies. They were more than I wanted to handle.

I wanted something that would grow monthly recurring revenue. I eventually narrowed it down to landscaping, cleaning, or automotive. These industries aren't about to be replaced by robots. Certain parts of the jobs may be, but you can't have a robot taking out trash and wiping desks down. At least not in the foreseeable future.

I had other criteria. Location: I didn't want to commute farther than an hour. Tenure: the company had to have been in business at least ten years. Employees: I needed at least two senior people in the company who had been there for five-plus years. These things, plus the potential to scale, were parameters I set when assessing businesses for sale.

I did my due diligence with researching various companies to ensure everything the business owners presented in their seller's packet was accurate. It was important to have access to their information in a transparent way so I could look over all areas and get an accurate read. I also placed great importance on being able to speak with their key employees, especially in smaller companies. If a business owner was reluctant to have me do that, that would be a red flag. Full disclosure of the financials and speaking to employees gave me the most critical information I needed to feel good about moving forward.

When I'd narrowed it down to ten companies, I traveled to the locations, and it amazed me how sellers represented themselves one way on the phone, but the in-person experience was completely different. Out of these ten people's places I visited, eight of them were in shambles just beneath the surface.

I met with one owner, and as I sat in his office asking questions, he shuffled through piles of papers on his desk, trying to locate information before finally telling me he'd have to get back to me. No thank you.

This discrepancy between what is projected and what was actual also applied to the financials. In many cases, when I did a deep dive, I'd find inconsistencies, missing information, inflated numbers, and other discrepancies that generated more questions. It's pretty typical to find skeletons in a business's financial closet. Spend the time you need to fully research a company—it can be the difference between financial success and ruin.

Eventually, I purchased CNS Cleaning Co., which met or exceeded all the criteria. As an added bonus, the owner had invested in marketing the company in a very limited way, relying on an unsophisticated website and word-of-mouth referrals. I saw that as an upside because I had marketing experience. I could apply my skill set to the company and expect success. I'm happy to report that four and a half years later, what I predicted came true, and then some.

If I ever purchase another business, I'll make a point to look at the client list. A huge portion of the business for the company came from government work, which is low-bid work. The only reason they got the job is because they were the lowest price. That gave them depressed margins, which meant they made very little money on that work, but it inflated the sale of their company because it looked as though they made a lot more money than they did.

# THE CNS WAY

Michael Gerber stresses the importance of being three people at the same time: the Entrepreneur, the Manager, and the Technician. One of his most recognizable quotes is, "The fatal assumption is that if you understand the technical work of a business, you understand a business that does technical work." Because I was so familiar with the E-Myth, I recognized right away the business we purchased had been run 100 percent by technicians.

I actually saw this as a huge opportunity for growth because while they were in the business of running the business, meaning they micromanaged everything, that meant they'd done zero strategic work in growing the business. To grow, the company needed to be run by an entrepreneur.

I began by talking to the current employees about changes. We told them what our vision was and what the company values were going to be. At first, they were all taken aback. The man who had worked as their VP of operations for ten years was a traditional manager, and he wanted to continue managing in the same way he'd always done. I worked hard to get him to see the business from an entrepreneur's standpoint. We would never grow if we continued to run things the same way. He had a hard time, as did the other employees, understanding the changes we were making.

They'd never been managed by someone with vision. We really shook things up.

But he's a smart guy, and he slowly came around to it because he also knew the previous owners had not been good managers. He was glad to work for someone who didn't yell and give ultimatums. I'm happy to say of the eight original employees, six of them are still working there.

In addition to that, there were two very good employees who had left CNS before we bought it who came back when they heard we took over. They told us they like working for someone who treats them well and pays them higher than a living wage.

My wife and I spent the first sixty days being technicians, learning the ins and outs of every stage, at every level. By the end of the third month, we shifted into the entrepreneurial role and started setting up systems and standard operating procedures. Having that hands-on knowledge allowed us to be more strategic in building an infrastructure that could handle scaling the business.

Setting up procedures has been the better part of what we've worked on for the past five years—we're still working on it today. It's a constant work in progress for us, because we're growing. And that's instilled in every single one of our people from when we start a new account to when an account closes. Everything is standardized and is done, as we call it, "the CNS way."

The previous owners had very few systems in place. There was no vision, no values, no creativity or innovation. Excel was the accounting system that managed their three-million-dollar organization. Again, I saw that as pure opportunity.

We've spent the past five years creating standard operating procedures for the simplest to the most complex situations. Having those systems in place has made a huge difference in our success. The employees aren't micromanaged because they know the system and are equipped with the information they need to take the next step.

We're very close to being able to open up a CNS in other markets outside of our geographical area, and have one or two people who can run our business for us and open up those new markets. We could replicate our Philly model in Boston, or San Francisco, or San Diego, and have everything online. It's a seamless, franchise model.

I tried to instill in the salespeople that when they are pitching our services, they can't sell on price. They have to tell potential clients what makes us different. Our goal is not to be the cheapest cleaning company out there; I don't want to operate that way. I coach them to focus on our customer service. That's what sets us apart from everybody else.

Whenever you call our office, even if it's midnight on a Friday night, you'll get a live person. If you call us Monday through Friday between eight and five, we pick up the phone before it rings three times. Whoever answers the phone will have a pleasant tone. If we owe someone a response, we get back to them in less than an hour. If we give someone a quote, we always get the price back to them in less than twenty-four hours; they don't have to wait two or three days to hear back from us.

So it's true, you'll pay a little more, but you'll get what you pay for.

———— • ————

If you're reading this and you've been successful working in corporate America most of your life, you are a great candidate for buying a business, if that's something you're interested in. You've gained the necessary skill set from your years of experience. Having said that, if you haven't found success working for someone else, I wouldn't recommend you leave to start your own business. Businesses have a higher chance of success when they're run by people who've been successful.

It is intimidating to read 80 percent of businesses fail in the first five years, but that number doesn't reflect the percentage of businesses that succeed if you purchase a company that is already successful. The percentage drops down to 20 percent.[1] That's a much easier number to swallow.

It's not all smooth sailing, and you'll definitely make mistakes and be humbled along the way, but I can say, without hesitation, it is worth it. I went from working a sixty-hour workweek with a three-hour round-trip commute to now working twenty hours a week. When we took over the company, in their best year they'd earned $3.2 million in revenue. After having the company for five years, we're set to bring in over $12 million in 2026.

The work I do now is entrepreneurial, though I spent a lot of time as the Technician and the Manager while getting the business up and running. Now I spend my work time thinking about strategy for growing the business.

The E-myth principles made all the difference by saving me a lot of time and helping me avoid common mistakes. Vision, strong values, and high standards are what our success is founded on. That's what it means to do it "the CNS way."

## ENDNOTE

1.    "Startup vs. Small Business: What Are the Differences?,"Maryville University, December 20, 2022, https://online.maryville.edu/blog/startup-vs-small-business/#:~:text=A%20report%20from%20Startup%20Genome,year%20%E2%80%94%20significantly%20lower%20than%20startups.

## About Bill

William "Bill" Dunn is the president and owner of CNS Cleaning Co. Since 1983, CNS has been the Delaware Valley's premier commercial cleaning company. CNS provides full-service commercial cleaning to thousands of clients each month across the United States.

Before CNS, Bill spent decades in the wine and spirits business, where he successfully recruited, hired, trained, and mentored future leaders. But Bill's ultimate dream was to one day own his own company, realizing this dream would take years of planning, preparation, and a commitment to hard work.

Bill knew a thing or two about hard work. He'd grown up on a farm, a farm his parents still work and own to this day. At nine years old, he mowed lawns, harvested hay, and helped care for neighbors' animals; then at fourteen, he started working at his father's truck stop. Bill took this strong work ethic with him into his professional life.

Despite his significant success in the corporate world, Bill knew as he approached age fifty that if he didn't make the jump into small business ownership, it would only get harder to leave. So in 2021 he and his wife, Kim, took the biggest financial risk yet when Bill left his management job and purchased CNS Cleaning Co. In the first two years under Bill's leadership, the business, based in the Philadelphia area for over forty years, has doubled.

In 2021 CNS had the honor of being selected to participate in the CNBC TV show *No Retreat*, where key executives from different businesses go through a boot camp that helps them team-build through adversity while also learning vital business practices. The show was heavily promoted on NBC and the radio program *Morning Joe*.

One of Bill's proudest accomplishments as owner of CNS has been helping others succeed. "The opportunities we've created for our partners have had a huge impact on their livelihood, which makes me very proud."

While the success is nice, Bill knows CNS can do more. As the company expands its reach, Bill and his team stay committed to the model that success comes when serving the customers' needs at the highest level. Built from day one to be different, CNS' experience, trustworthiness, and, above all, customer service set them apart from the rest.

To learn more, visit cnscleaningco.com or reach out to Bill directly at bdunn@cnscleaningco.com.

CHAPTER 6

# HONESTY, INTEGRITY, AND HUMILITY

*Building a Sustainable Business the Right Way*

By Michael J. Killen

I sat at the dealer award ceremony, surrounded by my team. We awaited the announcement of which business would walk away with the win. When they said our company name, everyone erupted in applause.

I clapped just as loudly and smiled just as brightly, but inside I quietly asked a nagging question: "What am I going to do?" Our company was selling a ton, but we were losing money left and right. I thought about the money we were spending on hotels for this ceremony and felt a pang of panic. I was a new father and constantly stressed about money and responsibilities, and I had no idea how to get my business under control. I thought about the college courses I'd enrolled in to learn my way out of the mess, and my mind started calculating those expenses. I was secretly pulling money from my savings to keep everything afloat, and I could see the quickly arriving and inevitable end.

This was also the year I met author, speaker, and coach Howard Partridge. I was invited along with a few other top dealers to see his presentation. When he offered the group spots into his Inner Circle community, my heart sank. I trusted Howard had answers that would untangle my business, but I wasn't sure I could afford the buy-in.

Feeling torn, I called my wife and dad to ask their opinion

55

on the investment. I'll be forever grateful for their support and encouragement.

I easily could have looked at the money alone and turned down the opportunity. Never had Howard as my mentor. Never been introduced to Michael Gerber's *E-Myth*. Never freed myself from the trap of my business and set myself on the path to freedom, peace, and fulfillment.

## CREATING MY OWN HANDCUFFS

In February 2004 I started working for a small shop that sold sheds and other merchandise from Amish country. I was coming out of a dark time in my life and was grateful for the work. Immediately I was enamored with our Amish suppliers. They lived and operated with honesty and integrity. A handshake was a binding contract, and I knew it would be honored because our relationship was built on loyalty and trust. I dove in headfirst and learned everything possible about the community and business.

After three years at the company, I had to walk away. There was a noticeable rift between the owners and seemingly everybody else. I'd had enough of customer complaints, lawsuits, and drama. The way the business was run, I was shocked it was still operating.

Even before I formally decided to strike out on my own, I had this recurring thought. What if we ran a fair business and just did what we said we would? It was such a simple idea, but I wasn't seeing that core tenet in practice.

One evening, I was driving down a busy road with my dad— one we'd been on countless times. When I happened to look up, I saw a big sign and felt like lightning had struck me. I told my dad to pull over. I'd seen a For Lease sign, and even though I still can't explain it, I knew without a doubt that spot was my store location.

I excitedly called the number the next day. The phone rang and rang. No voicemail. Just continuous ringing. I must have listened for five full minutes. I don't know why I didn't hang up, but eventually a voice arrived on the other end.

"Yeah, hello?"

"I'm calling about your property on Route 51," I said.

"We just put that number up there!" the man exclaimed. "What do you want to do with it?"

"Well," I replied, "I want to sell Amish-built sheds and furniture."

The man paused for a long second and then, in an amused voice, said, "I think you're going to make a million bucks there!"

At the time, I didn't have a lot of savings, but my dad lent me $10,000 to get started. It was a *huge* amount of money. We met the property owner and made the deal. After some bumps and false starts, Amish Yard was officially in business. We started developing relationships with Amish builders and growing the company.

But a problem lurked at the core of that business. I didn't know how to run it without my constant involvement. My desk was front and center at our original location, and everything went through me. I'd created this monster that was entirely dependent on me. Every customer question or business-related decision needed my input. When I went on vacation, barely an hour went by without a call from the office. In a way, it made me feel important. I was needed, competent, and knowledgeable, and I wore that like a badge of honor.

Then the cracks started to show. When I took time off for my son's birth, our sales went backward for the first time in company history. We were selling, developing relationships, and winning awards, but it all felt like a house of cards.

When Howard became my mentor and recommended Gerber's *E-Myth*, it was a difficult read. It painted such an accurate picture of me as the technician starting a company and failing to operate like an entrepreneur. When I embraced the book's lessons and Howard's roadmap for how to stop being a slave to my business, everything changed.

We created systems and processes within the company that allowed me to spend time with my family—while the business still grew. I didn't even know that was possible. By implementing what I learned and leaning on the support, encouragement, and accountability of my network, I no longer feel trapped by my company. I'm excited about my role, the new milestones we're reaching, and the time and energy I've freed for everything I care about outside the business.

# GROWING PAINS AND LESSONS: WHAT I LEARNED (FINALLY) BUILDING A COMPANY

All those years, I thought I was building a business. All I had done was make myself a job. A difficult, time-consuming, all-encompassing job. After shifting into the entrepreneurial mindset, I realized I could build something infinitely better using a few simple but key concepts.

### Stop working in your business. Start working on it.

The primary lesson I took from the *E-Myth* was the need to transition away from doing everything in my business. While the book suggested getting an office down the street, I couldn't quite go that far right away. I moved upstairs. It was a small step, but it got me out of the middle of everything. From there, I started incrementally taking myself off the schedule.

This idea of not being constantly in the office was entirely foreign. I didn't even know operating that way was an option. In those early days, I wasn't an entrepreneur in the true sense of the word. I wasn't creating opportunities, channeling a vision, and supporting others to thrive and grow.

Once I took that first step back, I had space and perspective to realize my constant involvement was actually holding everything back.

### Where procedures don't exist, chaos rules.

Implementing systems is critical for a thriving business. When we started, nothing was written down, formalized, or developed. Nothing was predictable. We were constantly being taken by surprise.

Then we got serious about working on our policies, procedures, and processes. Even today, we constantly refine and update them to match our current reality.

If you listen in on one of our meetings, you're sure to hear, "What's the procedure on that? What's the policy?"

## Overcome the fear.

Getting out of the way as quickly as possible is the only way to see your company sustainably, predictably grow, but I know from experience a lot of fear is associated with that. I'd built up these excuses around why I couldn't step back from the business. Even something as simple as moving my office seemed unthinkable. But as my mentor, Howard, says, "Faith over fear."

My company didn't see significant growth until I released that fear and started trusting the processes and others to do their jobs. This period of change was painful. We lost employees I couldn't have imagined losing. Then something interesting happened. We realized the company we were building *and* those former employees were all better off.

Later, opening another business location wasn't even on our radar yet, but after driving past a spot for lease, that feeling hit me again. I knew that space was our second location. I leased it before we even had employees to fill it. I definitely jumped and built my parachute on the way down on that one!

Change is difficult. But if we hadn't implemented those new policies, had that personnel shakeup, or expanded into that new office, nothing would have changed. It would have felt safe, but we never would have experienced the growth we saw.

Change is never going to feel right or comfortable. If you want to embrace growth, the best, most practical, most strategic time to start is now. Regardless of circumstances.

Yes, change is scary, but having a network of people to rely on, including my loving family, a dedicated leadership team, a trusted coach-mentor, and the Inner Circle community of other high-achieving business owners, provided me with invaluable support and accountability. I can't imagine weathering those changes without them.

## Establish your core values.

"You can have everything in life you want, if you will just
help enough other people get what they want."

—Zig Ziglar

Tenacious. Innovative. Caring. Knowledgeable. When we sat down as a leadership team, we decided these four core values were what made us tick in every sense of the word.

Caring was the first and most unanimously embraced, which wasn't surprising. Time and time again, I've seen every team member elevating others. Every day I see them asking the important question: How can I help everyone else? Customers and employees alike feel and respond to that genuine caring in our company.

Building leaders and empowering team members has been our proven path to collective growth and success. We've had many team members for over a decade now, and my proudest moments come from witnessing others' transformative journeys.

One individual, Rob Macsurak, comes to mind. After parting ways initially, we welcomed him back, and his journey of intentional personal growth has been remarkable. His transition into a leadership mindset fills me with immense pride, and I'm humbled by my role in fostering an environment where he could thrive.

The growth I've seen in our team is deeply gratifying, with each member's progress and triumphs worthy of their own narrative. Perhaps one day, their stories will fill the pages of a book, but for now, that's a tale for another day.

## Know why you're doing it all.

Sometimes it feels as if my entire life started with the birth of my son. Being a father awakened things I didn't even know existed within me. It gave me the inspiration and motivation to want to do better. My children, Jessie and Ryder, are six and seven now, and I can confidently say how quickly the time goes. Being able to be home and spend time with my family is everything. Having Fridays just for daddy day is everything. Being able to contribute as a soccer and T-ball coach. Participate in church activities and serve as an elder. In this season of life I can't put a value on that.

For the first ten years of my business, I was on call seven days a week, twenty-four hours a day. Now I get to spend more of my time and energy on things that truly matter to me. Knowing the underlying why behind all my actions means I never lose perspective or gratitude.

I recently overheard someone talking about a business he had owned and how he had hated it. The long hours. The draining demands. The inability to take a vacation. He said he eventually quit and got a job.

That easily could have been me. Had I not found a better way, I could have called it quits. I could have packed it all in for an employee position and never built this company that's now serving so many. I'm tremendously blessed that life introduced me to the right people and concepts and that I knew enough to listen to that wisdom.

## Learning what not to do is invaluable too.

I'm grateful I had the opportunity to work for that original company because it gave me additional clarity about my priorities and how I wanted to operate a business. It taught me what not to do.

I saw firsthand the consequences of acting selfish and being fearful, argumentative, and dishonest. I saw what happened when you told people whatever they wanted to hear and then never followed up or followed through. I saw the inevitable result of making all decisions around what's best for you and never your clients.

As a business owner, employer, and father, I try to do everything from a place of love. In all my decisions and actions, I strive to fearlessly advocate for others, and that has brought tremendous benefits back to me. When you stop worrying about your bottom line and start worrying about your clients, that's when your business starts to grow in surprising, wonderful ways.

**There's always hope, and change is possible.**

For many years, I couldn't imagine any real future for myself. My life today versus those dark times is a testament to what can be achieved when you operate with purpose.

No matter your situation, it's never too late for change. It's never too late to embrace gratitude, humility, and a genuine desire to be useful to others.

# THE BEGINNING OF THE CLIMB

My company still wins awards—recognition from the Better Business Bureau and commendations as one of the top places to work locally—but now there's no fear or angst when they announce our name. I'm not clapping along but secretly feeling stretched to breaking or wondering how to pay the employees next month. In that place is overwhelming pride for our amazing team and the system we've built that allows them to succeed every day.

After plateauing at three million dollars in revenue, we're now on pace to make eleven million dollars with three locations. This growth has happened with me working three-day workweeks during the summer and focusing on my strengths instead of trying to do everything.

Reading *The E-Myth* fundamentally changed how I thought about running a business. I suddenly had the knowledge and belief there was a different, more freeing, more rewarding path forward. I'm now also understanding that I'm obligated to share these concepts, and one of my core job responsibilities is to bring imagination, creativity, and fun. It's been so liberating working *on* my company these last years, and I know we're just getting started!

## About Michael

Michael J. Killen is the visionary founder of Amish Yard LLC, an award-winning company recognized for its exceptional outdoor products and outstanding customer service. Armed with over two decades' industry experience, Michael's journey began with a humble $10,000 loan from his father, which he transformed into a multimillion-dollar enterprise generating over ten million dollars annually.

Beyond his achievements in business, Michael has a passion for personal growth and development. As a Certified Human Behavior Consultant specializing in the DISC model, he possesses a deep understanding of human dynamics, which he applies both professionally and personally. Inspired by the Ziglar philosophy, Michael believes in the power of positive thinking and continuous improvement.

Michael's commitment to personal development extends to his role as a husband to Ashlee and a father to Ryder and Jessie. He cherishes every moment spent coaching his children in youth sports and guiding them through life's challenges. His dedication to family and personal fitness is evident in the time he devotes to nurturing his relationships and maintaining a healthy lifestyle.

Michael is deeply involved in his community. He finds joy and purpose in helping others, whether it's supporting business growth or aiding individuals in their recovery journeys. His compassionate nature and desire to uplift those around him make him a respected and beloved figure in his community.

When he's not busy with his professional or community commitments, Michael enjoys the peace and serenity of his nine-acre ranch. Surrounded by his family, he finds solace and inspiration in his rural retreat.

Michael J. Killen's life is a blend of entrepreneurial success, personal growth, and community service. His multifaceted approach to life and business, along with his passion for helping others, has made him a dynamic leader and mentor. Through his journey Michael continues to inspire those around him to strive for excellence and embrace the transformative power of personal development.

Learn more at
- MichaelJKillen.com
- AmishYard.com

# CHAPTER 7

# EXITING THE CAVE

By Mike Dusi

**M**y entire life has revolved around family and a dedication to hard work.

My father was the first one to show me and my brothers what hard work looked and felt like—and he did so right in the heart of Ozone Park, Queens, New York. Whether it was long hours in the pizzeria, the meticulous management of his real estate ventures, or his relentless commitment to our family, every detail mattered. Mom mirrored this dedication, treating every tenant and customer like a loving relative, while ensuring orders flew out perfectly. My life was a constant hum of activity: customers, tenants, family, neighbors—all surrounded by the relentless pursuit of getting things done (GTD). Dad, with his watchful eye—and sometimes with a belt at the ready—saw my boundless energy and helped turn it into a powerful tool. He taught me to channel it into hard work, preparing me to tackle all of life's challenges head on.

Back in my early twenties, my neighborhood was my kingdom, and I felt invincible. Blinded by youthful ego, however, I didn't realize there was an entire world beyond my familiar surroundings. Most people think the world they live in is the whole world. It's not.

Growing up in Queens, the myth was that you would end up dead, in jail, on the run, or making pizzas until you were cremated in the oven. However, I had big dreams, and I aspired for even greater achievements. I wholeheartedly believed the road to success was paved with a wild frenzy of purposeful, direct action.

I felt most comfortable when I was bizzy, bizzy, bizzy and doin' it, doin' it, doin' it—that always made me feel on the right track.

My passion for hard work blinded me to the chaos that could follow if left unchecked. Everywhere I turned, I was getting the same (false) narrative: "Work hard! Give it your all! Do it yourself to ensure it's done right. Sleep a little, then repeat." However, as I learned, if we don't work smarter, we end up working harder. John D. Rockefeller said, "He who works all day has no time to make money."

By God's blessing, I was born with boundless energy. Working on things that excite me only fuels my spirit even more, which makes me very...*unpredictable*. I'm one of the lucky ones that gets to do things I enjoy, and I do it with unlimited enthusiasm!

In the pizzeria, I was the ultimate technician, making the dough to keep things cooking. Later in life, it was managing dozens of departments and resources while producing multimillion-dollar movies in Hollywood. However, I was addicted to "being busy," and I simply didn't realize it. It wasn't until I ventured into real estate investing that I learned the importance of working *on* a business and letting it streamline itself as a true entrepreneur, rather than working tirelessly *in* the business as a technician.

However, as usual, I'm getting ahead of myself. So, like any good story, let's start at the beginning.

## HOW I BROKE THROUGH MY OWN MYTH

Many of us are pulled in by the myth and allure of the entrepreneurial spirit as a technician. The myth is that most businesses are started by entrepreneurs with tangible business skills. The reality, however, is that most businesses are started by technicians who are skilled at the actual job but lack the entrepreneurial tools and knowledge needed to keep and grow a successful business.

When I began my entrepreneurial journey, I—like so many of us—approached business with the mindset and determination of a capable technician—aka a doer.

You might say that I was born with the "entrepreneurial seizure" that Michael Gerber describes in his *E-Myth* books. No matter what business I was in, I always had the sense—deep in my gut—that I could do the job better than the people running the show. This was the source of my greatest accomplishments, but also my biggest obstacle.

Michael Gerber explains there being three roles in a business:

1. **The Entrepreneur (the visionary)** invents a scalable, system-driven business. They focus on innovation, growth, and the future, creating a business where others known as Technicians handle the work under the super-vision of managers, thus allowing the Entrepreneur to develop systems that enable the business to run inde-pendently of their constant involvement.

2. **The Manager (the organizer)** turns the Entrepreneur's vision into reality through effective planning and organizing. This role ensures the business operates smoothly day-to-day by creating and maintaining sys-tems and processes.

3. **The Technician (the doer)** is the hands-on worker who gets the actual work done. Skilled in their trade, they are responsible for producing and delivering products or services. This role focuses on executing tasks with expertise and maintaining high quality.

Myths aside, knowing how to do the work in a business has nothing to do with creating a business that works. The reason most businesses don't work is because the people who own them *do all the work.* Ray Kroc was the visionary behind McDonald's success. He focused on expanding the business rather than flipping burgers, transforming a single restaurant into a global, fast-food empire. He proved: *One doesn't get paid the big bucks in life for what they can do, but what they know and can get other people to do.*

Most everyone has a universal myth when it comes to running their own business: "If I become my own boss, things will get easier."

But they don't. They get harder. Much, much harder. We shouldn't just strive to become better at what we do; rather, we need to focus on creating an enterprise that replicates what we do so that other people can do it. We must put our personal highest and best value talents to use. Moreover, it is imperative that we work *on* the growth of our business, not just *in* it. Focusing on strategic planning—and building systems and processes that allow the business to flourish and operate independently of our constant involvement—is key.

"The system is the solution, not the people" is my mantra. But before you respond, "Some people are not replaceable, Mike," I can tell you that there are graveyards full of individuals once deemed irreplaceable. Having a system in place is crucial to ensuring the business doesn't collapse, regardless of who departs. The system will always be there for a new employee to follow documented instructions.

As Michael Gerber puts it, "If our business depends on us showing up every day, we don't own a business; we own a job, and we're working for a lunatic, ourselves!" Building a business that works predictably every time in the hands of a decent wage employee is the main goal, and systems are more valuable than anything else. Systems are the secret sauce to success. Pizza pun absolutely intended.

## THE DOING ZONE

I always felt my dad ran the neighborhood. Still today, he has a worldly, gravitational pull that the universe revolves around him, his plans, his ideas, and his actions. That's how it feels to me and anyone who knows him. He carries himself like the boss of all bosses. When I lived in Queens, he was an owner and a landlord in a neighborhood where most people weren't either. Everyone knew he had extensive expertise and a deep understanding of the restaurant business.

But what could Papa Johns, Dominos, and Pizza Hut possibly do that my dad and the over fifty thousand independent pizzerias in the United States didn't already excel at? What do these three big franchises do, even in this very moment, differently than all the other fifty thousand pizzerias?

They aren't making better pizza. They aren't better with customers. They aren't smarter or harder working.

Their massive yet *only* advantage is having operational procedures in place that make their product reproducible, predictable, scalable, and, most importantly, reliable to a loyal customer base who knows exactly what to expect every single time.

I couldn't see that back then. I was too deep inside the pizza cave, my family, and my neighborhood to know anything different. It was just like Plato's cave allegory, which describes that people resist new knowledge that challenges their deeply held beliefs. In the allegory, several prisoners are trapped in a cave, which they believe is the whole world, until one of them escapes into daylight. The escapee comes back to tell them all what he's found outside, but no one believes him. I was a prisoner in a cave, rejecting the insights of a freed prisoner.

Unsurprisingly, when this workaholic eventually left Queens for more chaos in Hollywood, I was still suffering from the delusion that hard work alone equaled success.

And don't get me wrong, hard work got me very far. As an actor, I quickly achieved success and earned accolades, but it was the producers on movie sets that I came to admire. They were the ones handling real business: extinguishing fires and making tough, last-minute decisions.

There is a difference between being addicted versus being committed, and I was addicted to the chaos. The gravitational field of it all was too strong. It was pulling me in. Soon, I was fully absorbed by the mayhem of a Hollywood movie set.

## THE ORGANIZING ZONE

I started working with producers and became known as the go-to guy for getting things done. "Mikey the mountain mover," they soon called me. I did everything from negotiating vendors, to booking travel accommodations for cast and crew, to hiring and firing, and everything in between. I became the ultimate *hatchet man*.

When something absolutely needed to be handled, "Give it to Mikey!" they'd yell—and I would get it done.

I was in my twenties. I had no idea about systems or processes. If you've never been on a movie set, you've never seen a system like it. Land, sea, air transportation, hotels, food, cast, crew, equipment vendors—there are a million moving parts.

Every piece must be thought through, and every detail affected the entire production ecosystem. On a movie set, I had to maneuver people and their equipment to locations according to a schedule dictated by a very strict budget, all surrounded by very large and unpredictable personalities.

I learned all the procedures and protocols. And over time, I learned about systems. This was my moment of transition from technician to *manager*.

The day before one production, our TV show pilot producer demanded to renegotiate terms and threatened to withdraw support. My partner and I refused, fired everyone involved, and found replacements within two hours. Our established system and network kept the production on track, proving that systems, not individuals, are the keys to success and freedom from difficult personalities.

If my previous work as the technician existed in the *Doing Zone*, I was now fully a manager in the *Organizing Zone*, but I still wasn't seeing clearly. I remained in the cave, working too deeply in the systems themselves to understand what it meant to really own something that was scalable and repeatable—something that could build real wealth without my daily involvement.

Warren Buffett said, "If you don't find a way to make money while you sleep, you will work until you die."

## THE AUTOPILOT ZONE

"There is nothing so useless as doing efficiently that which should not be done at all."

—PETER DRUCKER

Coined by educator Laurence J. Peter, the Peter principle states, "You can only rise to the level of your own incompetence." And in business, it is omnipresent, touching every aspect of our work and lives. This is why it is mandatory to be constantly learning.

Throughout all my adventures in the movie business, I always dabbled in real estate deals. When I told people I wanted to do it seriously, everyone said, "Get a real estate license." However, to this day, I've never done one deal with a license. Rather, I jumped into investments, where I've done over five hundred deals. If a myth is something people feel they know to be true but isn't, then my experience qualifies. The myth of needing a license was useless.

Recently, while playing with my daughter on a sunny day at my Malibu beachfront investment property, I overheard my partner take a call with a prospective client. In six minutes, I identified how he effortlessly used over twenty calibrated questions and strategies to close the deal. When I asked him about it, he said he wasn't even conscious of the techniques he used. This is the essence of mastery—being unconsciously competent.

## The Dunning-Kruger effect describes the four stages of competency:

1. First, you're **Unconsciously Incompetent**: You are unaware of what you don't know, so you can't recognize your own lack of knowledge.

2. Next, you're **Consciously Incompetent**: You become aware that something exists but don't know how to do it, which makes you enthusiastically useless.

3. Then, you become **Consciously Competent**: You are competent in the task but can only do it through intense concentration.

4. Finally, you become **Unconsciously Competent**: You are so skilled that you no longer have to think about what you're doing; this is mastery.

Becoming a real estate investor was the moment in my life when I transitioned from managing systems to overseeing and benefiting from them as an *entrepreneur*. I progressed from the *Doing Zone*, to the *Organizing Zone*, to the *Autopilot Zone*.

With the very best technologists Silicon Valley has to offer, I recently built an AI digital framework system for my investment firm that replicates mastery techniques for real estate transactions, all leveraging generative AI and deep learning.

Currently, I'm embracing a mindset of saying *no* to doing and *yes* to systematizing. While chaos still tries to pull on the strings of my life, it no longer has a full grip on me. I once said *yes* to everything, but I've learned that sometimes there is far greater value in saying *no*.

As I soak up the sun out here in California, I've had a good deal of success staying out of the cave that once held me captive. And that brings me to a newfound goal: helping to break my friends out of the cave's darkness and encourage them to come out in the light with me. We owe it to our future selves, our families, and our businesses—and we owe it to the next generation.

I believe in living out the example one aspires to be. Don't just be a doer. In fact, rather than making a to-do list, create an anti-do list. It identifies and eliminates unproductive tasks that detract from your primary goals, helping you focus on what truly matters and enhancing your productivity. In the words of Lao Tzu, "Doing nothing is better than being busy doing nothing."

We've only got one life to live, and the choices we make daily determine whether we will spend it staying busy in the cave of doing or bringing systems to life in a world of true, illuminated entrepreneurship.

I know where I want to be. What about you?

## About Mike

**Entrepreneur | Real Estate Investor | Film Producer | Business Thought Leader | Best-Selling Author | Mentor**

Mike Dusi is a multifaceted entrepreneur, a film producer, an investor, and a best-selling author who exemplifies the principles of scalable business models, efficient systems, and the fusion of innovation and practicality. Mike has spent more than twenty years transforming ideas into successful enterprises, challenging conventional wisdom and focusing on systematic growth. To date, Mike's reputation spans overseeing high-budget film productions to revitalizing distressed properties. He has a keen ability to view each endeavor as an integrated system, where the people run the processes and the processes drive results.

In his versatile career, Mike has made significant contributions across the film, real estate, and entrepreneurial business sectors. His film expertise spans domestic and international film production, from high-budget features to commercials. He has overseen productions in six countries and nine US states, mastering all phases of filmmaking: development, financing, production, and distribution. Mike's agility in balancing creative vision with practical execution has earned him respect and admiration among peers, clients, and audiences. Though much of his success stems from strategic agility, it is all a by-product of challenging the status quo of business systems, a theme deeply explored in Michael E. Gerber's *The E-Myth Evolution.*

Mike's accomplishments are heavily rooted in viewing his business as an integrated system, where efficiency and scalability are carefully connected. Driven to inspire others, Mike is also an elite keynote conversationalist, a distinguished TEDx speaker, and a televised interviewee across multiple continents. He advocates that true business success comes from creating systems that allow businesses to thrive independently of their founders, demonstrating the potential that rises from working on the business rather than in it.

Mike's philosophy aligns with Michael E. Gerber's principles of business, advocating for continual innovation, quantification, and orchestration. This mindset focuses on building enterprises that operate independently of the founder's constant involvement.

A native New Yorker with Kosovar Albanian roots, Mike spent his formative years in Queens, New York, before moving to California in 2003. Now residing in Los Angeles, he cherishes time with his wife and children while continually evolving his business systems and workflows to drive success for himself, his team, and those whom he inspires. To Mike, learning is something that is never finished.

# CHAPTER 8

# HUSTLE MUSCLES AND BUSINESS MODELS

By Phil Nahajewski

When I turned thirteen, I went through the rite of passage for kids in my working-class Detroit neighborhood. I got a *Detroit News* paper route: Deliver about forty papers every day, collect the money on Friday, pay for your papers on Saturday, and get to keep ten dollars profit. Not a bad little gig in the late 1960s.

So when I was offered a route twice the size, I figured I had hit the big time, doubling the income of all my paper delivery friends. That was when, long before I got my MBA from the University of Detroit, I learned a fundamental business lesson: always look a gift horse in the mouth (or as my future CFO self would say, do your due diligence).

Because if something seems too good true, chances are it is. My extended route, I found out, covered Detroit's notorious 8 Mile Road and centered on the trailer park that was featured in rapper Eminem's gritty 2002 movie of the same name. Many of my customers in that low-income community were, let's say less reliable or amenable than those living in nicer parts when it came to handing over their payment at the end of the week.

Talk about getting an early taste of some of the challenges of entrepreneurial life, my first attempt at collecting from my customers on Friday only covered half the sixty dollars I had to pay the *Detroit News* the following day. I realized early on that I was going to have to work a lot harder than my buddies if I was going to make any money. I had to hustle. I had to make multiple trips to the trailer park on Saturday to be able to pay my bill, and then make extra trips throughout the week to track down my non-payers to generate a profit.

Thankfully, this started the development of the "hustle muscles" that would become an important part of my future success as an entrepreneurial-minded CFO.

## SEARCHING FOR A FUTURE

When I was old enough to get a job on 8 Mile that paid $1.60 an hour for pumping gas, it was less stressful than chasing down payments from *Detroit News* customers and it helped me save enough money to live in the dorms of Michigan State University for a few years. I struggled with deciding on a career direction, though. I eventually noticed it seemed to impress women when I told them I was planning to go to law school. That line worked with a beautiful young woman I met in a bar when I was twenty-two, and we're still married forty-seven years later.

Anna and I started a family during our second year of marriage. I found a job as a cost accountant for a plumbing manufacturer in Detroit near Wayne State University, where I was attending law school. We bought an old house near 9 Mile and Woodward for $25,000. Paying for the house, Anna's pregnancy, and law school tuition was overwhelming. My hustle muscles were in full use as I attempted to juggle being a cost accountant, family man, and law student. I knew that I had to find a better job to survive.

Six weeks into law school I got an offer from the largest non-automotive company in Detroit—the Burroughs Corp., then the second-largest computer mainframe company in the world. Only IBM was bigger. The position came with college tuition reimbursement—a financial game changer for me.

It also became a career game changer. The tuition reimbursement did not apply to law degrees, so I dropped out of law school and decided to pursue my MBA from the University of Detroit.

Another factor in my decision to switch career direction was something I realized while observing the general counsel and the chief financial officer at the plumbing manufacturer. In football terms, the general counsel seemed like a special teams player, brought in when his specific skills were needed. The chief financial officer was in on every play, working with every facet of the business (sales, operations, administration, and more).

I wanted to be in the action like that: I now aspired to become a CFO.

## RIDING THE TURNING TIDES

Those hustle muscles I developed as a paperboy and later as a struggling family man served me well as I began my corporate career with Burroughs, a two-billion-dollar computer mainframe company that became a five-billion-dollar company during my first eight years there.

Competition for the plum assignments that could propel a career was fierce. I relied on my entrepreneurial mindset and outhustled my peers to advance. When assigned to manage an accounting department, I viewed myself as having a "department-reengineering business." I was relentless in getting my projects done.

After a few successful department reengineering efforts, I earned a promotion to a controller position. Now I envisioned I was running a "performance-driving" business. The company's controllers were statistically ranked every month and results were widely shared. I hustled my way up the monthly rankings to earn a prized spot in the Top Ten percent for the two years I held this position.

Then, our five-billion-dollar company acquired another five-billion-dollar company (Sperry) to form Unisys, where I was picked to serve on the integration team. These were heady days. It was a great ride until... Two disrupters named Bill Gates and Steve Jobs exited their garages and attacked the computer business with a better business model that shifted computing power from the data center to the desktop. We were obsoleted quickly. The great Unisys merger of 1987 became known as the "mating of the dinosaurs" the following year.

The Unisys team was loaded with talent that had built up their hustle muscles during the industry's glory days. But we all learned together that hustle muscles are not enough when you're disrupted by the likes of Microsoft and Apple. That effort needs to be coupled with a business model that can disrupt and outperform your competitors.

It was time to leave a sinking ship for what was a rising rocket—the cable TV business. Time Warner Cable recruited me to be the lead financial executive on a team that was integrating cable systems acquired across western Ohio. It was exhilarating to create a new organization from the businesses owned by four different companies, and a wonderful opportunity to combine my hustle muscles with an innovative and powerful business model.

Cable TV was using satellites and coaxial cable to deliver dozens of channels to a world that was previously only viewing CBS, NBC, and ABC. When our cable TV business model was disrupted by satellite services like Dish and DirectTV, we upped our game, spending billions on a new fiber/coax network that could deliver hundreds of channels while also disrupting the phone companies whose twisted pair of wires could only deliver mediocre DSL service to homes and businesses compared to our high-speed internet service.

Five years after helping to create Time Warner Cable's Western Ohio Division, I was tapped to help launch its new South Carolina Division, formed from five separate acquisitions. In my entrepreneurial mind, I was now in the organization-creation business. Our business was thriving as we found new ways to leverage our powerful business model.

When the new millennium began, I jumped at the opportunity to become the lead financial exec for Time Warner Cable's Tampa Bay Division, an established operation with over one million customers and one billion dollars in annual revenue. My hustle muscles continued to get stronger as I did my part to drive financial performance. Our division had the highest percentage operating cash flow growth among the company's forty operating units.

Another opportunity to create a large new organization surfaced in 2004 when Bright House Networks spun off from Time Warner Cable. I was named the lead financial exec for a newly formed two-billion-dollar Florida Division and helped the new owners shift the new company's culture toward a more customer-focused, longer-term approach.

Those were more glory days, but I learned once again that they don't last forever. Change was coming anew, this time in the shape of the internet. Cable's video and advertising revenue began to go to upstart streaming services like Netflix and YouTube. Once more, simply working harder couldn't stem the turning tide.

## HELPING THE BOOTSTRAPPERS

When my twenty-year run in the cable TV business ended, I found myself with a fat severance package and a hunger for a new challenge. The first was to become a CFO for a financially distressed nonprofit. Early in my cable days, I'd had the opportunity to apply my CFO skills to help rescue a similar financially distressed organization in Ohio. I was glad to have the opportunity to replicate that rewarding experience in Florida.

A chance meeting with a founder of a tech startup made me realize how much I missed the adrenaline rush of creating new businesses and building new brands. This person had a brilliant idea for a business model but lacked the funding to build out the innovative social media software needed. We worked side by side to raise eight million dollars in capital. An experienced CFO was exactly what the founder needed to build investor confidence.

The tech community in Orlando, Florida, soon learned of this success and began inviting me to listen to their pitches. I loved it. I clearly caught the "tech startup" bug. Over the next decade, I earned shares and/or options in ten tech startups whose founders impressed me with their hustle muscles and high-potential business models.

I rejected more opportunities than I accepted, though, as I also met more than my share of what I came to call dream chasers. These were people with good ideas but without the discipline needed to see them realized. I was looking for the boot-strappers—those with hustle muscles who were out to show the world how much they could achieve with small injections of capital.

Along the way, I have learned that tech startups are like roller coasters except for one thing: Roller coasters usually stay on the tracks!

## SHARING WISDOM AND BEST PRACTICES

Though I didn't call myself a fractional CFO at the time, I can now see how I evolved into one as my career progressed. As the lead financial executive for billion-dollar divisions of Time Warner Cable and Bright House Networks, I was providing experienced financial leadership to a diverse mix of operations and businesses—such as plant construction, installation, field service, network operations, call centers, B2C sales and marketing, property solutions, business solutions, advertising sales, and local programming channels. It felt as if I were the CFO for a dozen different teams at a time.

Later, simultaneously serving as the CFO for a variety of tech startups, I found I really loved the diversity of helping many different teams. Accumulating different skills and knowledge and regularly bringing best practices from one company to another has made me a better CFO.

I was attending a venture capital event in St. Petersburg, Florida, in 2019, hoping to find investors for a few of my favorite tech startups, when I unexpectedly found the business model of my dreams. I met Don Noble, a partner in the Florida CFO Group, a group of eleven experienced CFOs in the Tampa/St. Pete market looking to expand into the Orlando market.

I was skeptical at first. I had been approached previously by other CFO groups and was unimpressed by their business models. They typically had agency models that inserted a middleman between the CFO and the business owner who needed their services. After working for CEOs and division presidents for the previous three decades, working for an agency did not appeal to me.

The Florida CFO Group was different though. I realized that its non-agency model attracted the best CFOs by providing them with the freedom, flexibility, and fellowship that they crave. I accepted the invitation to become their twelfth CFO partner and launch their brand in Orlando.

Today, The Florida CFO Group has grown to over thirty experienced CFO partners. Our secret sauce is that we are seasoned executives who love to share our knowledge and experience with each other to help our partners better serve their clients.

It's a beautiful business model: I get to do what I love—helping businesses with my CFO talents. I get to do it my way, using my experience to determine what's best for each client. And I get support from the best CFOs who love to share their expertise.

I enjoy the diversity of helping a variety of businesses in a variety of ways. I've been a fractional CFO for companies across the spectrum—from making cement, fences, ice cream, and beer to developing software, celebrity branding, and emotional intelligence training. I've helped businesses dig out of financial holes, solve people problems, execute strategies to scale to new heights, and exit at favorable valuations. It's been a rewarding experience collaborating to make good things happen.

## VALUING THE HARD TIMES

An additional reward of being a fractional CFO is how it has allowed me to allocate my time between making good things happen for business owners and doing other things I enjoy. It's given me the opportunity to explore new fun things.

In recent years I have tried standup comedy (at charity events), creating a YouTube channel (the Florida Entrepreneur Success Network), becoming a talk show host (CFO Coffee Talks), and getting a little crazy with my speaking engagements for Disrupt HR, a human resources forum. For one talk I impersonated Elvis interviewing for an HR manager job. For another I had a friend choreograph a team of "Let's Get Fractional" dancers to dress up like Olivia Newton John and dance to the tune of her hit "Let's Get Physical."

I recognize that all I get to be part of now is due to some of the rougher times I've experienced, for which I have a deeper appreciation. The trailer park on 8 Mile. Early financial difficulties as a family man. Working for companies getting disrupted. Serving to rescue financially distressed nonprofits. These were the seasons that put my hustle muscles to the test. And just like the way our bodies' muscles get stronger from workouts, hustle muscles get stronger when you use them. My hustle muscles were a big part of making me the CFO that I am today.

Much like the golfer who needs to find new ways to win a hole as their age takes yards off their drive, wise old entrepreneurs need to shift from reliance on hustle muscles to the discovery and development of their business model. As Michael E. Gerber has observed, it's not about working smarter rather than harder. It's about working harder and smarter—combining muscle hustle and business models.

## About Phil

Phil is a CFO with over forty years' financial leadership experience across a wide range of enterprises. He served as a financial executive for large technology and media companies (Unisys, Time Warner, and Bright House Networks). He was the top financial executive for Bright House's multibillion-dollar Florida operations.

He has led the rescue of three financially distressed nonprofits as a board member and as a CFO. He has helped ten tech startups in a variety of roles (CFO, investor, adviser).

Phil now serves small and midsize businesses as a fractional CFO. He became the first Orlando partner of the Florida CFO Group in 2019. He founded the Florida Entrepreneur Success Network (FESN) in 2020, which produces *Meaningful Minute* videos in which experts and entrepreneurs share their advice.

Phil has an MBA from the University of Detroit and is a frequent volunteer for nonprofit boards and mentoring programs. In addition to being an experienced CFO, Phil likes to step out of his comfort zone and try new things, such as being a YouTuber (https://lnkd.in/eF9z34z), a standup comedian, an Elvis impersonator (https://lnkd.in/gNAQGisw), and a LinkedIn Live talk show host (CFO Coffee Talks) for the Florida CFO Group.

# CHAPTER 9

# LEADING WITH HEART

By James Thomasson

*"The more I lead with my heart, the stronger it gets. The glass is always completely full—half air and half liquid. Leaders are dealers in hope. Believe in your ability to create."*
—MARK MILLER

I want to tell you about one of our clients. We'll call him Charlie, mainly because that's his name.

I'd been doing Charlie's taxes every year since 2003 when I bought the West Mobile location of my accounting business. He came every tax season, like clockwork, for us to prepare his taxes, and he always seemed to leave the office as a happy client. Until one year when Charlie just...didn't show.

It does happen, rarely, that a loyal client will leave my firm for a season or two, but they usually find their way back. Charlie was no exception.

I ran into him between tax seasons. "James," he said (desperation in his eyes), "I really need to see you."

"Of course." I told him. "Anytime."

A few weeks later he was in my office, documents in hand. He told me he'd decided to do his own taxes the previous year. "I saw how easy you made it look," he said, "I'm a smart guy, so I thought I could probably do it myself." He looked down, sheepish. "After three hours of frustration, I decided paying you was worth it."

As an accountant, I hear this story a lot. "I thought I could do it myself." I don't blame anyone: hiring an accountant is an investment. If you've got a simple return—because you're a W2 employee without any complicated assets or deductions—doing an online tax return probably isn't a bad idea. But if you're a business owner, chances are you're going to be leaving money on the table if you try and manage it yourself.

I finished Charlie's return and gave him the bottom line: He'd be getting a $983 refund. His face went funny.

"Are you sure?" He asked. "My information is very similar to last year's" (the return he did himself), "and last year I owed $1,472."

"Well, let me look at it again," I said. I've been doing small business taxes for thirty years, but even I sometimes make a mistake. I went through his return, line by line. Nope, all was in order. Charlie was owed a $983 refund. I asked him if I could look at his return from the year prior. The one where he owed $1,472. Right away I found a suspicious figure. "Where'd you get this number?" I asked him, pointing.

He shook his head. "I didn't understand the question," he said. "I plugged in what I thought was right."

I handed him back his return. "That right there," I told him, "Was a $2,462 mistake." (which we promptly corrected by filing an amended return for him).

As he left my office that day, he told me that from then on if he had tax returns to file, I would be preparing them. No matter what.

Charlie made that $2,400 mistake because he had fallen prey to a common small business owner's myth: "I can save money by doing my own taxes." Sure, you could save money by doing your own taxes. You could also save money by developing your own software or building your own office space or shooting your own commercials. But if those things aren't your area of expertise, it's probably not going to turn out very well for you.

We learn, when we're building our businesses—as Michael Gerber illustrates so well in the *E-Myth* series—that our strengths matter. It's human nature to make assumptions about what we can do: "That doesn't look too hard. I'm a smart guy; I can figure it out." But assuming expertise isn't the same thing as *having* it.

When you get that "entrepreneurial seizure," as Michael calls it, you must learn everything you can and be a student of your own game. Once you know your strengths, your weaknesses are hard to hide. You have to hire professionals and other experts to fill out those weak spots. In a word: no matter what your business, you need a team. It's nearly impossible to scale without a good one.

I've always put a lot of value in the people around me, so I've always done my best to keep close those who have a quality or expertise I lack, and then invest in training and educating them where they have their own gaps in knowledge.

Take Kari, for instance. She's been with me for thirteen years. When Kari first started, she knew almost nothing about accounting. But I could tell she was smart, and she had a fierceness that I don't possess. Her brand of take-no-prisoners loyalty was exactly what we needed at the time, all those years ago, and now she's my right hand.

In fact, this writing wouldn't be possible without her. She's in the room as I type, making suggestions and demanding I not forget details.

Kari is why you need to build your team. There are several employees who have been with me as long or longer than Kari. Bonnie, for example, has been with Accelerated Accounting since I bought the firm in 1995. That's over thirty years on the same team.

Employees like this have been the backbone of my business. They've stayed because they love what they do, and because I try my best to make them feel like they work *with* me, not *for* me. I know that if I can give them the guidance and skills to keep things running smoothly, then I can stay focused on the big picture. I can continue to work *on* the business, not in it.

You can't grow a pie business (to steal a metaphor from the first *E-Myth* book) if you're sweating it out in the kitchen from morning until night. Someone else needs to do the baking so you can focus on growing the business. Hands flour-free.

# MY OWN KIND OF PIE

I started doing my own tax returns when I was in high school. Back then we did all our returns by hand. I was young, and my needs were uncomplicated. One year, however, the local community center in my town (in Mobile, Alabama) asked if I could come do some cleanup work. Their regular janitor had left or gotten sick; I can't remember which.

I had gone to preschool at that community center and had fond feelings for it, so I agreed. That year, the City of Mobile sent me my very first Form 1099. I had been doing fine with my own taxes up until then, but the 1099 made me nervous. I was now a "sole proprietor" in the eyes of the IRS, so I went to H&R Block to get a professional's opinion.

The preparer looked through my scant documents. She asked me what my state refund had been last year, and a red flag went up for me. "I don't need to give you that number," I told her, "because I didn't claim it as a deduction the previous year."

She nodded. "Oh, right," glossing over her mistake.

That little error would become the spark that sent me on my own path toward entrepreneurship.

Before my "sole proprietor" work at the community center, I had been slinging bags at a local grocery store. I was the sixth of seven kids, so we all got jobs early. Of my siblings, I was the only one to finish college. People had been telling me all my life that I should be an engineer. I was good at math and had an engineer's mind for tinkering, but when I got to college, the coursework just didn't thrill me. I transferred early on to the business school. We had a saying at my college:

The engineering school graduates come out crying, "We have jobs!" The business school graduates come out saying, "Working for *us.*"

Several of my brothers were entrepreneurs, and it seemed like a good route. They had independence and were making good money. When I graduated, I found a job at a bank. All the while, friends and family who knew that I had a knack for numbers kept coming to me to do their tax returns. It started to feel like maybe a business was coming into focus.

In addition to the example of my brothers, I also felt that I had what it took to be an entrepreneur. I knew that I could work hard, but more than that—I knew I could work smart.

In my job at the bank I would notice how quickly things would start to build up on my desk. Tasks that only I knew how to handle. I realized quickly that if I was going to make any headway, I would need to empower the people around me to help. That lesson stuck with me when it came time to build my own firm.

You can't cling to every task in your business. You can't walk around with the mentality that you do it best, and no one else is going to live up to your standards. If you do, you'll get burned out, and no matter how well you do, it won't be enough.

I have a competitor who feels very strongly that everything must pass through his desk before it can go out to clients. When I lock up and head home for the night, he's still in his office, working away, checking all the boxes. Most nights he's there until ten or eleven. That's not a sustainable business model.

To be successful, we all eventually have to ease up on control and let other people be the technicians. Not only will this put you in the position to scale—freeing up your time to create the systems and processes you need to meet customer expectations and keep the business humming—it will also make your employees feel seen and recognized as the essential parts of the business they are.

# PEOPLE FIRST

As Kari will tell you (and is urging me to write down, right now) my biggest strength and biggest weakness are one and the same: my heart.

Our company is family first. That means if an employee has someone or something to take care of in their personal lives, we make sure they have the time and space to do it. *You take care of your people.* That's a philosophy I was raised with and won't ever abandon. A couple of years ago, Kari had a family emergency. She called me on the way to the hospital and told me she wouldn't be in; she didn't know for how long. Turned out, she had to stay home and take care of that family member for the next eight months. During that time, we made sure she never missed a paycheck. We figured out how she could work from home, long before WFH was the norm.

It doesn't matter whether it's one of my longtime employees or a brand-new-to-us client, if there's an issue that we can help with, we will. We never charge widows for tax returns the first year after the death of their spouse. We work with our clients who have suffered any kind of loss to make sure that the work gets done on their behalf, without additional burden.

My employees stay with me because they know that I care. Same with our clients.

Do people take advantage? Occasionally, but that's why I've got Kari. She'd defend this company to the bitter end, and she keeps her eyes out for people looking to capitalize on our compassion. Eventually, it all works out.

I believe that it's better to be good people and good stewards of all the gifts that God has given us than to only be focused on profit. Profit can't be the only driver. You need a mission, some larger goal for yourself or the company, to motivate you to keep going. In the early years of Accelerated Accounting there were times during the offseason that I had to get another job so that I could keep paying everyone's salaries.

If my only goal were profit, I would have abandoned ship in those tough times. Instead, I always knew that I wanted to have a positive impact on the people and community around us. That kind of mission keeps you going when times are lean.

# LEADING WITH HEART

After all these years, my most prized possession isn't a house or a car or a watch; it's a plaque that was given to me by my employees. Every year as tax season draws to a close, we have an end-of-season party to recognize our collective strengths. We hand out plaques for things like "Most Tax Returns Completed." Three years ago my employees got together to make a plaque for me. It had been a hard year, and they wanted me to know that they noticed how much I was doing on behalf of the business, and them.

The plaque reads "World's Best Boss." My name, James Thomasson, is written underneath, and then a quote:

> "A good boss makes his men realize they have more ability than they think they have so that they consistently do better work than they thought they could."
> —CHARLES ERWIN WILSON

They tried to pick something that would be meaningful to me, and they got it exactly right. To make my people (you'll have to forgive the antiquated use of "men" in Mr. Wilson's original quote) feel that they can do more and be more is one of my ultimate goals as a business owner and leader.

Some people believe you must push and push to get what you want from the people who work for you, and that the only trade worth making is dollars for effort. I don't subscribe to this way of thinking. I truly believe that long-term growth comes from taking care of people.

We're not the most expensive accounting firm in our area. Even though we have a niche—small business accounting—there are others who charge more for the same services. We keep our prices where they are because we have a full plate of loyal clients. We don't need to advertise; we're known and referred.

I've been blessed to create a business where no one works for me. We all work together, with the same goal in mind: to serve the people around us, and one another, and to grow *together*.

There are bigger and wealthier businesses out there that might turn up their noses at this kind of philosophy, but I believe that if you're trying to build something that's authentic to who you are, compassion is the best and quickest road. If you're interested in building more than a business, something you can look back on as a true legacy for yourself and the future, you need to lead with heart.

## About James

James Thomasson is an accomplished and forward-thinking accountant, consultant, and entrepreneur, as well as the president and CEO of Accelerated Financial Services Inc. and a best-selling author of *Success in Any Economy*. With an extraordinary career spanning several decades, he has consistently demonstrated his ability to think outside the box, delivering innovative solutions and driving business growth.

Before developing Accelerated Financial Services Inc. to what it is today, James served as the president and CEO of TBS Communications Inc., where he led the company to new heights of success through his visionary leadership and strategic acumen. His exceptional skills in financial management and business development have earned him a reputation as a trailblazer in business.

In addition to his corporate responsibilities, James also serves as the chairman of the United Bank Advisory Board, where he provides invaluable insights and guidance on financial matters. He previously held the position of chairman of the Saraland Area Chamber of Commerce, where he played a pivotal role in fostering economic growth and strengthening the local business community.

James' journey toward excellence began by working his way through college and earning a bachelor of science degree in finance from the University of South Alabama. He started his own accounting practice in 1987, and since then his entrepreneurial spirit has driven him to acquire ten different tax and accounting practices, establishing himself as a recognized authority on business acquisitions.

Throughout his illustrious career James has consistently proved himself to be a visionary leader with a deep understanding of finance, business strategy, and the art of successful entrepreneurship. His passion for innovation, coupled with his extensive knowledge, has positioned him as a sought-after expert in the industry. James Thomasson's dedication, expertise, and unwavering commitment to excellence have earned him the respect and admiration of his peers and colleagues alike.

# CHAPTER 10

# MASTERY AND MISSION

*Mimosa Salon Suites and the Path to Love*

By Douglas Hauptman Jr.

I was talking to my chiropractor like he was my therapist. As he twisted and cracked and released, I poured out my business woes. I was starting to buckle under the weight of my responsibilities, and it was all palpable, there in the back of my neck. He pounded on my shoulders. "You're all locked up," he said.

I had recently opened the doors on my most recent business venture: Mimosa Salon Suites. Ten thousand square feet of office space in Conyers, Georgia, that had been converted into individual salon suites to be rented by beauty professionals. The goal of the business was to provide a landing pad and a place to grow for lower-income business owners, primarily black women, most of them in their mid-twenties to mid-forties.

Our occupancy was full, we were doing well and growing, but I was single-handedly managing every aspect of the business. It felt to me as if everything in the company relied on me. When I tried to outsource, it was ineffective because no one seemed to care as much as I did or perform to my standards. I wasn't sure what to do, but I knew if something didn't change, I wouldn't be able to sustain.

My chiropractor looked at me and my hiked-up shoulders, and he presented me with a gift.

"Here," he said. "Read this."

He handed me his phone. On it was a book, *Awakening*

*the Entrepreneur Within: How Ordinary People Can Create Extraordinary Companies*, by Michael Gerber.

I left his office, my back feeling much better, and ordered the book as soon as I returned home.

I should back up for a moment and tell you that I've always been an entrepreneur. I started at the age of seven, with a lemonade stand on the corner of 35th and MacArthur Boulevard in Oakland, California, where I grew up. I chose 35th and MacArthur because it was on one of the busiest corners, across the street from a bus stop. Even at seven I knew a thing or two about supply and demand.

I grew up, and in my early adulthood I caught the wave of the technology boom of the 1980s. I ran a company that sold microprocessors and semiconductors to some of the biggest computer manufacturers of the day. It was good business, but not great for my soul, and was eventually pulled out from underneath me in a hostile takeover.

From there I moved into marketing, and then to real estate, which is where I germinated and eventually built the idea that became Mimosa Salon Suites. I was no beginner, and I'd done plenty of things right, but it wasn't until I read *Awakening* that I realized how much I was still doing wrong.

I had built a business on my own faltering back. I hadn't yet created the systems or innovations that would allow me to step out from under all the daily tasks and truly begin to grow.

I've always been a reader, and a self-taught man, so I began to implement Michael Gerber's lessons immediately. *The E-Myth* had changed my mindset in a single reading, but it was just the beginning of a larger shift. Like any transformative book or set of ideas, it was a catalyst rather than an endpoint. I went on to read *E-Myth Mastery: The Seven Essential Disciplines for Building a World-Class Company* next. Others followed.

What I understood right away is that I would need to learn and become an expert in all the different areas of my business. The *Seven Essential Disciplines* became a blueprint for how I could begin to have true mastery over this thing that I was building. I did what I always do: I began. I put one foot in front of the other. The spirit that kept me hawking cups of lemonade when I was seven was the same spirit that I brought to growing my business: "I'm not sure if this is going to work, but I'm going to give it a try."

It's the song of the self-made person. It doesn't matter if you're the smartest or the fastest, if you can stay the course and stick it out, even when things get tough, you're going to go the distance. I dug in. I started studying and researching and learning. I read every other *E-Myth* book I could get my hands on, as well as many other books on the areas I needed to grow into. As I progressed, I found two key lessons to be the most pivotal in taking my business from one ten-thousand-square-foot location to three locations making almost one million dollars a year in revenue.

## LESSON ONE

I needed to have a mission far larger than the success of the business, and after working through the exercises in part 1 *of E-Myth Mastery*, I came up with our mission statement: "One Million Square Feet of Hope!"

I'm no stranger to missions. When I was young and on the heady cutting-edge of personal computers, I tasted a kind of financial success I'd never known before. I had tens of millions of dollars in contracts, and I was living the high life, in every sense of the word. Though it had its thrills, there was an emptiness to what I was doing. I, and everyone around me, was motivated entirely by the almighty dollar. I was rich, but I wasn't sleeping well at night.

I understood, without anyone ever telling me, that the road I was on might lead me to a vast fortune, but it wouldn't take my soul anywhere but down. It was when I left that world and started building websites as a contractor that the first seeds of *mission* were planted.

I still remember the church service I went to, just months before I started Mimosa Salon Suites. I was making in the high six figures at the time, and the sermon was about how those of us with wealth needed to find ways to give back. It hit me hard. After leaving the world of big tech, I had encountered my spiritual self and developed a deeply personal relationship with God. I understood how much of the health and goodness of my current life was due to that union, so I took the sermon seriously: I was supposed to be a good steward, using what I'd been given to make the world a better place.

I sat in the pew and made the decision. I would find a way to do something sustainable that would provide a service to people in the world who needed help and support. Reading *The E-Myth* all those many years later reminded me of the importance of my original mission.

The goal of your business can't be the profit. If it is, you'll lose sight of what matters and quite possibly who you are and what you stand for.

The goal of your business must be the community you'll serve, the changes you will bring, and the hearts you plan to set aflame.

I wasn't just renting salon space; I was helping people become entrepreneurs. With that in mind, I began to focus on all the ways in which we could support our tenants so that if they wanted to, they could grow into business owners themselves. Today, every new tenant in any of our Salon Suites locations gets a free copy of *Awakening the Entrepreneur Within*. We've created online courses about business development that we offer free of charge to our tenants. Instead of trying to trap people in a lease, we have a seven-day cancellation policy. We also offer a three-week break from rent for maternity leave, one week for bereavement, and prorated rent for any kind of hospital stay. We're one of the only in our industry with these kinds of policies in place.

If our mission were pure profit, we would act like 99 percent of the other landlords out there and hold tenants captive until they finally managed to squeak out of their grasp. This kind of predatory practice, at its core, just isn't good for business.

It turns out that being compassionate, and just doing the right thing, *is*.

The men and women who rent from us are fiercely independent and quite motivated. They're sick of being gouged renting a chair at a larger salon, where they have no freedom and no right to the profits of any products that they sell. They want something that they can call their own, and that's what we provide for them. In most cases when one of our tenants leaves, it's because they are starting their own salon or shop.

Most landlords hate the move-out notice from a tenant, but for me it's cause for celebration. Many of these people have become an extension of my family. I've coached them when they've asked, supported their aspirations in whatever way I can, and watching them walk out the door toward their own business venture fills me with pride. Not that *I* did any of it, mind you; it's all their own drive and determination that got them there—but it always feels like an honor to have provided them with a place to start.

And because our practices are built on compassion, support, and growth, there's always another tenant ready to fill their spot.

## LESSON TWO

*Awakening* will get your mind set in the right direction, and *Mastery* will set you on the path to growth. As I began to learn about all the disparate areas of the business, simultaneous to building our mission, it became clear that understanding the ins and outs of the business was the only way out of the trap of "doing it all myself." I taught myself sales and marketing and operations. I learned the needs and pain points of our tenants. I figured out what was missing and then found the people and processes to fill those gaps.

The results of this work were undeniable. We went from $200,000 in revenue to $950,000 in revenue over several years, maintaining a healthy 50 percent margin with the eighty-two units we run at

100 percent occupancy. Because of the systems now in place, we have our eye on big growth by way of franchising.

Because of my tech background, I understood that we had to leverage technology in every way we could to create systems and processes that work. For time and project management we use Basecamp. For surveys we use SurveyMonkey. For social media planning and scheduling we use Hootsuite. Most recently, we've begun adopting the AI strategies from AI marketing platform deal.ai. You can't have a true enterprise if you don't have enterprise systems in place.

I also made sure that we had a built-in innovation loop in place. That means that innovation is an active, trackable part of the systems of the company. We aren't just maintaining the status quo; we are constantly evolving so that at any given point in time, we are at least a step or two ahead of our peers and competitors. The COVID-19 pandemic was a great example of this. By February of 2020 I saw the writing on the wall. I was one of the first business owners in Atlanta to write the initial medical protocols for the pandemic. These later got woven into the state policy. I understood that it was our job to create an environment where people both *felt* safe and *were* safe. We accomplished it, and because of that planning and innovating, Mimosa Salon Suites were able to stay open throughout most of the entire pandemic.

These are just some of the ways in which building true mastery will help you survive. Very few businesses do. Creating a business plan that reflects your values and building your own deep understanding of your organization and its systems will separate you as a survivor, rather than just another flash-in-the-pan.

As I learned and stretched, I documented every part of the business we were building. At this point, many years into this learning, I am confident that if I were to disappear tomorrow, my business could run successfully without me. That's how ingrained and teachable every process is. I've also created a succession plan, and the youngest of my four children, my daughter Mali, is set to learn the business and one day take over. To my great pride and joy.

This groundwork also supports our next step, franchising Mimosa Salon Suites. My "One Million Square Feet of Hope" dream is to see a Mimosa Salon Suites in every city in the country—wherever there is need—so that aspiring salon owners can have a place to build their own future. I've seen the impact we've had on the community here in East Metro Atlanta, and I know the need is deep and far-reaching.

As we execute our franchise plan and wait for the ideal economic timing (another lesson of mastery), I'm busy growing and coaching. I've realized that I, as the face of the business, am an integral part of its continued success. A system of my own. So I have prioritized my health and well-being, to grow right along with the business. I believe that by building my own brand, I can reach beyond my tenants and colleagues to touch the hearts of other business owners and entrepreneurs—especially those of my own generation. Because getting older doesn't have to mean sitting in a chair on your porch, watching the world go by. Aging is not what it once was. I'm sixty-three years old, and I have no plans to slow down anytime soon.

Michael Gerber, now eighty-eight himself, often gets asked if he's going to retire. His answer is always *no*. Why would he? If he's taught us anything, it's that when you're building something great, living your dream, and aligned with a mission larger than yourself, there is no need to stop. If you're lit up with what you're doing, all you want to do is keep it going.

As I get older, my mission comes into even sharper focus.

I'm here to build bridges for aspiring entrepreneurs. I'm here to encourage and to coach and create opportunities. But more than anything, I'm here to love. To find grace and compassion and forgiveness wherever it lives.

So many of us look to our differences instead of what we have in common. Creating Mimosa Salon Suites has shown me how alike we all really are, and though I may not have known it at the time, it was love that motivated the creation of Mimosa Salon

Suites from the very beginning, and love that will keep it going, growing, and innovating.

Once you find *that*—the love that powers your goals—then you know you're on the right path.

## About Douglas

Douglas Hauptman Jr. was born in Los Angeles and raised in Oakland, California, except for the time he moved to San Diego for high school and junior college, where he studied business and psychology at Grossmont JC in La Mesa, California. A lifelong entrepreneur, he started his first business, a lemonade stand, at age seven on the corner of 35th and MacArthur Boulevard in Oakland.

He began several business ventures in the '80s in the information technology area and never looked back. Ups and downs along the way allowed him to see the different sides of business deals, and he decided early on to never take or offer a bribe or do any other thing that he knew was unethical or immoral. He often shares that "life's about choices, and there's rarely time to make sure they are all the right ones. Don't waste any time worrying about getting to where you really want to be. Just go for it. Stay open-minded and vulnerable to the things you really need and were meant to be for."

When it comes to putting things in order in Doug's life, priorities are God, family, and country. He never loses sight of the many gifts and blessings he's been given. He uses his talents as an actor, model, coach, property manager, mentor, digital marketer, teacher, and REALTOR® to actively promote justice and equity in every effort and engagement. He often jokes that he's at the same time a mutt and the truest of North American royalty! Yet he's most certainly proud of his many different heritages, including Scottish, Black Irish, Welsh, Viking, and Cherokee.

His current focus is on Mimosa Salon Suites, which rents affordable salon suites to beauty professionals. With locations in markets where the need for economic opportunity is in the greatest demand but the lowest supply, Mimosa has an eighteen-year track record of helping economically disadvantaged persons pursue and achieve their passions for serving others.

Mimosa Salon Suites developed a first of its kind training and tenant success platform that actively engages and helps people learn and practice the different business skills needed to succeed in today's competitive market. Mimosa University provides the community platform for all this to take place. Having started three locations, Doug seeks to engage with other like-minded businesspeople to launch 150 more to create "one million square feet of hope!"

For more information, visit https://hoo.be/doughauptman.

# CHAPTER 11

# THE PIZZA GUY

By Michael Fomkin

I got my start working in the dish pit at Al's pizzeria. Where I grew up in Brooklyn, New York, pizza was a big deal. Working at Al's meant I was learning one of the best on the block.

Al believed in making a quality pizza. In fact, he made it his personal mission to give every customer that came through his door the best pie imaginable. He made certain that everyone felt like they were right at home.

He spared no expense in ingredients. Whether it was tomatoes for the sauce, mozzarella cheese, or a specialty item like shrimp, he always got the best. Al was a good steward too. I remember he would always share ingredients with his competitors if they ran out of something.

Not too long after starting at Al's, I moved up from working in the dish pit. The boss had taught me the ropes and moved me up from dishwasher to making pizzas. Soon, I was managing the place, running the show, just like he taught me to.

Customers weren't content to choose Al's pizza over the other neighborhood places. They also wanted him to personally make their pie for them. Whenever they would see me stretch out the dough, or ladling the sauce, the customer would almost inevitably lean in and say: "Hey, I want Al to make mine."

Looking back, I feel pretty lucky to have learned the ropes from someone who people looked at with such fondness. For someone of my impressionable age, Al was a terrific mentor. But in order to maximize my success, I had to learn a different way to do business.

# THE APPLE PIE GUY ... ONLY PIZZA

Being a good guy from the old neighborhood, the recognition Al received for his pizza making gave him a great deal of satisfaction. Whenever one of those regular customers would walk through the door and ask for him by name, I remember he would stop what he was doing. However important the task, he would put it down and make their pizza for them. It didn't matter what else he had to do, paperwork or heading out on his way home, Al was in the pizza business for two reasons: he enjoyed making people happy and he loved making pizza.

Back then, there weren't a lot of career options on display in Brooklyn, New York. In the neighborhood where I grew up, you either grew up to be the guy that hung around the bar, became a cop or a fireman, or got a job as a union laborer. When it came to making your own way in the world, there weren't a lot of role models to follow.

I knew that I didn't quite fit in with any of the lifestyles I saw out on the street. I played sports, youth baseball and hockey, but that wasn't my thing. Beyond being a voracious reader, always at home in the stacks of the public library, I couldn't see another path for myself. Working for Al in the pizza business, I found something I was good at.

When I was twenty-one years old, I changed directions. I got into the restaurant business for myself, buying my own pizzeria. I took every lesson that I learned working for Al in his place, deployed some guerilla marketing ingenuity, and my place turned out to be quite a success for a whole. Then something similar happened to me.

Once I established my reputation as offering some of the best pizza in the neighborhood, customers started walking through the door with a similar request. "Hey, Mike," they would say to me. "Would you make my pie for me?"

For a while, I got a similar feeling Al did. I experienced joy. But even more than the immediate thrill of recognition, I felt overcome with an obligation to serve every one of my customers. Al was one of the best in the business.

Once customers started asking for my handiwork, that meant we had something in common. When you've gotten so good at making a product, especially something beloved like a pizza, recognizing people asking for you by name, has a tendency to blind you.

It didn't take long before I burned out on the restaurant business. Working the long, hands on hours, became quite a grind. Even though I had accomplished the entrepreneurial goal of running a successful business, earning a great reputation in the neighborhood, I looked for a way out. Running a pizzeria the way Al taught me had turned me into the 'apple pie guy'.

Al had taught me everything he knew about what he was fantastic at: making the best pizza. But what he didn't teach me, most likely because he wasn't aware, was how to think bigger. How to apply the framework to my business where I could work myself out of the day-to-day grind of the operation.

Al had made me the manager of the restaurant, which bought him some time off. But on the day I left, he had to go right back to making pies again. After selling my pizzeria, I looked at what my next step could be. I swore to myself one thing: I would never again create a business where people asked me to make their pizza.

## ENTERTAINMENT

After escaping the restaurant business and vowing to do things differently, I got started in my next career in an unexpected place: entertainment software.

The internet was still in its formative stages. Few people could see its full potential. I started working with a fledgling company that created software for on-line profiles for actors and actresses. I realized right away that this company offered a valuable service. Before the internet took over, aspiring talent distributed critical materials like headshots and profiles in physical form. Making connections was an arduous task. In show business, in order to get somewhere, you had to know someone.

Using the software our company created, clients could post their headshots and profiles more efficiently. On the other side, producers and directors could search a massive internet database filled with talent they could sort by specific criteria.

There was value on all sides. Not only that, there was limitless potential for growth. I invested everything that I had in it. Unfortunately, the company soon broke up in a massive, money laundering scheme. The scandal was all over the news. One morning, I received a phone call out of the blue, telling me that the company was bankrupt. Just like that, the bubble popped.

The call left me devastated. I operated ten offices. I held many lease contracts and employed five thousand people; the scandal left me high and dry. But instead of throwing in the towel, I stayed the course. I paid every one of my employees, honored each lease I had signed, and made sure that all of my customers that had paid for a service received fair value. It was the right thing to do. Unfortunately, doing the right thing left me almost broke and, even more discouraging, unsure what to do next.

## NEW OPPORTUNITIES

In the wake of that disaster, I did not know what my next move was going to be. But if you're looking for opportunity, it can sometimes rise out of what feels like the end of the road. From the ashes of that awful scandal, a potential bankruptcy, the seeds of my next company took root.

For a while, I had been kicking around the idea of creating a series of networking events. My earliest vision for these events was to bring prospective talent, young actors and actresses, together with established figures in the industry. We could provide a proper solution for the most troublesome part of making it in show business: connection.

Looking back, on the surface, the idea seemed rather audacious.

I didn't have any direct entertainment business experience or industry contacts (I had only been a software guy at the time of the scandal) but I took the leap anyway. What did I have to lose? I was going to host a networking event. My first event would be small, a hundred and twenty-five people, others from the industry. I just wanted to see what would happen.

I wrote and posted a Craigslist advertisement. I offered anyone willing to attend some compensation, access to talent and a hot lunch. Not sure what would happen, I went to bed. The next day, much to my surprise, I had received forty responses. It was more than enough industry interest to host the event I had envisioned.

My first thought was that people in the industry must be desperate for a hot lunch. But what it taught me was that I could write some pretty strong copy. From that Craigslist ad, and the resulting event, the earliest iteration of my present company, VIP Ignite Live, was born.

Eighteen years later, I still work with ten of the forty people that responded to my advertisement. Our clients have won thirty-eight prestigious awards, including six Tonys, received an array of accolades for their work, and produced films for streaming companies.

Our clients, at baseline, create connections. Those connections increase our profile, giving us proximity to people. From the start of knowing no one, we now work with real life changing influencers, making our company the proof of concept that a person can network their way into new and vibrant chapters of their entertainment career.

Even though the concept worked, our success was not instant. We struggled for a long time, part of which was living the E-Myth. We were doing everything ourselves. I went to every event from Comic Con to charity functions myself, doing everything I could to get proximity to people. For the first ten years, we had to ask if we were going to make it. But our unending drive to succeed, commitment to people, have brought VIP Ignite Live to where I'm confident enough to say that we are good at what we do.

I have found the benefit of simplifying the day-to-day function of my business. Free of the operation side, I could finally step back and see the bigger picture.

We have a team of skilled professionals for everything we do in VIP Ignite Live. We use those teams relying on a crafted system of frameworks and standard operating procedures. These structures give them a welcome sense of autonomy, which allows me to replicate critical aspects of my business again and again. We hire the right people for our positions, some of the best in the world at what they do, and give them the tools they need to succeed. Having vetted those SOPs, I'm able to trust that they can succeed without meddling with their work.

By removing the hands-on elements of my job, I can also step back and get a basic understanding of what's happening from a bigger perspective. I can, for example, look at what our media buyers and ads people are doing. When I plan something, I can create dynamic, high concept media solutions, trusting that the implementation is handled.

When you're always hands on, trusting the process can be difficult. I imagine Al felt that way with making pizza. But in the long run, by removing yourself, the business can provide so much more value.

## GROWING BEYOND OUR BOUNDARIES

Over the past few years, VIP Ignite Live has grown and expanded into exciting new things. We're focused on high-level business concepts such as lead generation, automations: creating systems, messaging, and relationships that work.

The confidence to continue on this growth trajectory, to push through devastating events like the COVID pandemic, comes from two concepts: having robust systems and giving people good value for their money. Those systems gave us the confidence to pivot from live events to Zoom, keeping us afloat.

Gathering everything I have learned, I am ready to embark on a brand new adventure where I envision helping entrepreneurs learn the art of storytelling in our new company VisionCraft. It has been amazing to come full circle and now feel empowered to pass on the lessons I learned to the next generation of business owners. In Hollywood there's a saying that it takes twenty years to be an overnight success: I did it in eighteen years, so I guess I arrived two years early.

I owe Al a debt of gratitude for what I learned at the pizzeria. Create a great product. Give the people something they will come back for again and again.

That's the value. Nothing works without that.

But I also learned something critical after walking away: how to separate myself from that product. It was difficult, but in order to achieve success, you need to ensure that the value the customer gets comes from their connection to the experience.

Not from their perceived connection to you.

## About Michael

Michael Fomkin's multifaceted journey through entertainment, business, academia, and philanthropy epitomizes a quest for excellence and profound impact across diverse arenas. With nearly two decades of experience, he has been a driving force in forging vital connections within the entertainment industry, guiding models, actors, and musicians through its intricate landscapes. As a forthcoming author, his upcoming book, *Elevate Your Message: The Hollywood Framework to Unstoppable Offers*, promises to redefine paradigms in talent development.

Among his literary accomplishments stands his number one best-selling book on Amazon, *Finding Fame: The Insider's Guide to the Entertainment Industry*, a testament to his insights and industry acumen. Collaborating with luminaries such as Mark Victor Hanson and Brian Tracy, Michael extends his reach into empowering individuals across various spheres, exemplifying his commitment to sharing knowledge.

Michael's speaking engagements, shared with luminaries such as Russell Brunson and Tony Robbins, have generated over one billion dollars across live and virtual platforms, earning him esteemed accolades such as the 10x Award from ClickFunnels. His academic pursuits, including a doctorate in system dynamics at MIT, mirror his thirst for knowledge, while his theatrical achievements, including six Tonys, showcase his creative finesse.

As the steward of Truth Mgmt, Michael fosters talent in television, film, and fashion, offering bespoke training and agency for aspiring speakers. His prowess in brand development and talent empowerment, recognized by *Forbes* and *Entrepreneur* magazine, demonstrates his enduring influence.

Beyond his professional endeavors, Michael's commitment to philanthropy shines through his contributions to Operation Underground Railroad and efforts to combat homelessness. In leisure, he indulges in art and rare books, reflecting his intellectual curiosity and cultural appreciation.

Honored with the Lifetime Achievement Award from New York City, Michael's legacy as a trailblazer in fashion and theater is firmly established, cementing his status as a visionary leader.

Connect with Michael: viptalentconnect.com.

# CHAPTER 12

# SMART BUSINESS EXIT STRATEGIES

By Geoff Green

H e looked at me with a big smile and a confident wink.

"My son's going to take over the business."

His words hung in the air, brimming with optimism and the weight of generations past.

But as a business exit strategist with several decades of experience, I knew all too well that such assumptions are often precarious, fraught with unseen complications.

I also knew his son didn't share his outlook.

Carlo was a second-generation Australian of Italian descent who owned a thriving real estate agency, originally established by his father after moving to Australia from Italy in the 1950s. A charismatic and strong leader with five children, Carlo viewed his business as the beginning of a family dynasty.

His eldest son, Santo, was a committed, industrious and gentle man. He had worked in the business for years and been designated by Carlo as his successor. I was well-acquainted with the entire family, particularly Carlo and Santo.

The passing of the so-called baton, though, strained their relationship -- with one another and with me.

I was having lunch one day with Carlo when he began to share his enthusiasm for Santo succeeding him in the business. I listened patiently. The company could expand, Carlo said. It could diversify, he added.

And then he smiled and gave me that knowing wink.

I took a deep breath, chose my words carefully and spoke.

"Carlo, I'm not sure Santo really wants to take over the business. I'm also not sure it would be the best thing for you, your family, or your business if he did."

My gentle words landed like a spark in dry grass. Carlo exploded.

He glared at me with intense anger for a full, prolonged minute. Then, abruptly, he stood up, leaving his half-finished meal on the table, walked over to the counter, slammed down a hundred dollar bill, and stormed out without a word.

Thankfully, Carlo and I reconciled. But even if we had not, I had completed my job with integrity and his best interests at heart. I had told him the truth.

Such is the life of a business exit strategist—an area I first started working in some 40 years ago. Eventually, I founded my own company, GRG Momentum, dedicated to guiding business owners through the complex process of transitioning from their companies.

Businesses are the engine of a free-market economy, and business owners are the innovators and risk-takers who make it all possible. They pour their blood, sweat and tears into building their companies. They hire the first employee and sign the first paycheck. They expand, and then expand again. They weather economic downturns. They adapt to technological changes. Quite often, they built their business not for a bigger paycheck but with the goal of developing better products or services to serve their communities and, by extension, the world.

As I discovered, though, too many business owners lack sound exit strategies, which means the future of many companies is in peril from the moment the owner retires, sells or steps down.

It's vital that companies continue to flourish once business owners exit. Otherwise, they are like magnificent structures that took years to build, but topple to the ground into worthless rubble once the architect steps away. And that, in turn, can have a direct negative impact on employees, suppliers and customers, as well as the economy at large.

For over a decade, the well-regarded Exit Planning Institute in the U.S. has been producing insightful reports on business owners' readiness to exit their ventures and the challenges they face in achieving successful transitions.

I find two sobering conclusions from their reports always stand out: up to 50 percent of business exits are involuntary and often less than 30 percent of businesses that go to market actually sell.

This is consistent with my observations working with clients over many years. The experiences of two particular clients are indelibly etched in my memory.

# ONE TOUGH TRUCKER

I'd known Max for years. He was as tough as nails, and you had to be in the trucking industry.

He was a larger-than-life character, with a huge, booming voice. While a bit gruff at times, he was always full of energy and enthusiasm for his business, family and life. His business had been profitable for many years, created jobs for his extended family and provided a good life for Max and his family.

One day I walked into Max's office to find him slumped in his chair, looking exhausted and completely defeated.

"What's going on Max?" I asked quietly. After a long pause he answered: "I just can't do it anymore. I haven't bounced back from my heart surgery last year and I'm exhausted. It's time—time to sell the business." I looked on in shock as a single tear ran slowly down Max's brown, weather-beaten cheek.

I had tried to have this conversation with Max for much of the last decade, and the blunt truth is Max should have sold his business at least five years earlier. Since then, his industry sector had changed, and with it the value and attractiveness of his business to potential buyers.

# THE DEAL MAKER

We were only an hour into the meeting, and already I could see Steven's head was spinning. The dark, wood-paneled boardroom of the top-tier law firm was rapidly feeling oppressive.

Lined up on the opposite side of the large oak boardroom table were a number of executives from the public company looking to buy Steven's business and a swathe of lawyers and accountants.

Steven was a brilliant, charismatic, fly-by-the-seat-of-his-pants entrepreneur. A natural deal maker. "I've done plenty of deals, how hard can it be to do an exit?" he kept saying to me in the weeks leading up to this important, initial meeting.

Not surprisingly, the potential buyer and its advisers were very well-prepared.

After a couple more hours, it was clear to Steven he wasn't going to sell his company for anywhere near his expected price, and the process and terms would be horrendous.

To his credit, Steven terminated discussions with the potential buyer a couple of days later, and we spent the next year preparing him for a highly successful exit.

# THE UNCOMFORTABLE TRUTHS

Stories like those of Max, Steven, and Carlo are all too common in the business world. Unfortunately, they each fell for what I call the "uncomfortable truths" of business exits:

- Your business probably isn't as valuable as you think.

- Most business owners aren't ready for their business exit.

- Good business exits take much longer than you expect.

- You often have little control over the timing of your business exit.

- Kids don't want to take over the family business anymore.

In addition, many private businesses are owned by baby boomers—and a virtual "tsunami" of baby boomer sellers is fast approaching as they head toward retirement.

# STRATEGIC EXITS

I've always been fascinated by the interaction between innovation and business. Few things are as inspiring as a talented, innovative entrepreneur working tirelessly to realize their vision. My interest began soon after law school, when I joined a corporate law firm and became immersed in high-stakes mergers and acquisitions.

I quickly gravitated toward entrepreneurial businesses, those run by business owners with the biggest visions and prepared to take the biggest risks. They were the ones who were either losing everything or—more often than not—striking it rich. Some called them lucky, but my gut told me the best entrepreneurs knew what they were doing.

As I worked closely with countless entrepreneurs, I discovered common threads running through the phenomenon of high-value business sales, sometimes referred to as "strategic business exits." This experience gave me unique insights into how great entrepreneurs develop and safeguard "exit value" within their companies, and how they subsequently execute highly successful exits. I've had the fortune of playing key roles in more than three hundred business exit transactions and have learned unique lessons from every one.

I've also had the opportunity to apply these insights to businesses I've invested in as an active early-stage investor, director and strategy consultant which, in turn, has helped me fine-tune my business exit strategies even further.

Eventually, I wrote a book about it—*The Smart Business Exit*—with the goal of helping owners of businesses, big and small alike, develop better strategies for exiting their businesses successfully.

# THE SMART BUSINESS EXIT STRATEGIES

Here are my seven strategies for achieving a successful business exit:

### Strategy 1: Have a real and enduring purpose.

One day you'll be pitching your business to potential buyers who will want to know why they should buy your business. If you can succinctly explain your business's purpose, what it does, and how it operates, you'll be far ahead of many other business owners in pitching to potential buyers.

### Strategy 2: See the future.

One of the key features of great businesses is their remarkable products or services. They also have an uncanny ability to introduce new products at exactly the moment customers want them. This ability to "see the future" often starts with a visionary founder. Embedding this mindset within a business is a hallmark of many of the world's leading companies: Think Steve Jobs at Apple and Elon Musk at Tesla.

### Strategy 3: Develop growth drivers.

Businesses with a clear purpose and remarkable products or services are always appealing to potential buyers. Even more attractive, though, is a business equipped with "growth drivers"— features that allow a new owner to quickly boost sales. This could be valuable intellectual property, a strong brand or a disruptive business model. Incorporating them can significantly enhance your business's value to prospective buyers.

### Strategy 4: Build to sell.

Most business owners believe their business is healthy; potential buyers, though, often disagree. Buyers want assurance that they can fully benefit from the business's value while minimizing their risks. A "build to sell" strategy addresses these concerns with two main goals: (1) develop your business in a way that secures and maximizes its value to potential buyers, and (2) organize and operate your business in a manner that allows you to transfer its full value to buyers with minimal risk.

## Strategy 5: Always think like a buyer.

Success in business often hinges on understanding your customers and their needs. The same principle applies when selling your business. Buyers ask a host of questions, including: Will the key staff stay? Are the customers loyal to the business or to the seller? Will we be able to integrate the business easily into our own or will it be a costly and time-consuming process? Are we paying too much?

It's essential to consider what your business really looks like if you stand in a potential buyer's shoes.

## Strategy 6: Get the best exit.

Unfortunately, most business owners do not secure the best deal when they exit their business; often they don't even manage to get a favorable deal. The key to a good deal involves four elements: (1) choosing the best time to sell, (2) appointing a quality advisory team to offer you counsel, (3) creating a competitive sale process, and (4) obtaining good deal terms.

## Strategy 7: Act with focus and urgency.

Focus is vital in any business, especially when your goal is to create value by developing new products or services, where the temptation to scale back during challenging times is greater.

Urgency is equally important. In today's highly connected world, you are likely not the only one thinking about or developing a new product or service. Often, being the first to decisively enter the market can determine the leader in new product or service categories.

# THE MINDSET OF A BUSINESS OWNER IS CRITICAL

The single most important factor in whether a business thrives or fails to develop is the mindset of its owner.

For millions of business owners worldwide, the most important advice they have ever received is Michael Gerber's sage, timeless advice: Work *on* your business, not *in* it. When a business owner truly embraces this advice, it fundamentally changes the mindset they bring to their business: how they create, develop and operate it.

I always tell business owners: Work on your business, not in it. Treat your company like you would a child, raising it to become independent and self-sustaining. One day you'll hand it off to someone else—to a family member, to your management team, or to an external buyer.

Systematize your business and then go on a holiday for a few weeks—to the beach, to the mountains, or to your favorite European resort. Then, and only then, will you know if your business can operate independently of you, and, consequently, if it can be smoothly transitioned to a future owner.

# THE ULTIMATE END GAME

Every business owner will one day exit their business. It's like death and taxes—it's an inevitable part of business life.

The mindset you bring to your exit is just as important as your mindset in creating, developing, and running your business.

Michael Gerber describes this well in his later book, *Beyond The E-Myth*: Your purpose as a business owner is to create and grow your business for sale to a new owner who can take your business to the next level.

It's also important to think about what your ultimate end game looks like when you exit your business. From discussions with hundreds of exiting business owners, I believe it has three key elements: freedom, legacy, and a renewed purpose.

With a well-planned exit and the right mindset, you can gain more freedom with your time, your finances, your hobbies, and your family. A thoughtful exit can help secure your legacy—what you have contributed to the world through your years of sacrifice. Lastly, it should open the door to finding a renewed purpose. Business owners often transition into new business projects, community involvement, and philanthropy after a successful exit—and tend to be highly effective in these pursuits. It's your choice.

Business owners employ your neighbors and sponsor local events. They transform society through their products and innovations. Without them, a local economy shrinks and eventually, dies. When business owners grow their businesses and exit successfully, everyone benefits.

Remember Carlo? About a year after he stormed out of our meeting, Carlo invited me for coffee at our usual cafe in North Carlton, a gentrified suburb in Melbourne's northern inner city.

"You were right," he told me. "My son Santo didn't want to take over the business."

His story had a good ending, though: Five years later he successfully sold his business, and he and his wife, Maria, achieved the retirement they desired. They also got to spend extra time with their kids and grandkids. Carlo had a good exit.

His story isn't uncommon. While many business owners *are* unhappy with their exit, an increasing number are finding success, thanks to good exit strategies, planning, and a lot of determination.

They win. So do the rest of us.

## About Geoff

For over forty years, Geoff has worked as a business adviser, corporate lawyer, and active investor with entrepreneurs and founders of high-growth and innovative businesses.

His work focuses on building strong enterprise value, preparing businesses and owners for exit, and achieving highly profitable business exits for founders and their fellow shareholders. He also has extensive experience with boards, advisory boards, and similar roles.

Geoff has held senior roles with several of Australia's leading law firms as well as the Australian Securities & Investments Commission. He has also played a key role in the development and ultimate sale of innovative private businesses such as BSX, an alternative stock exchange, and Fliteboard, the world's leading electric surfboard company.

He established his business advisory practice, GRG Momentum, over twenty years ago to help entrepreneurs develop strong enterprise value and achieve successful business exits.

Geoff has a reputation for bringing a high-quality, focused, and commercially pragmatic approach to business with a strong emphasis on strategy and execution.

He is a strong strategic thinker and a good facilitator, and has a well-developed ability to work through complex commercial issues in a clear, cooperative, and well-reasoned way. In addition, he has a finely tuned awareness of the emotional issues entrepreneurs often need to work through when exiting their businesses.

Geoff is the author of the highly regarded book *The Smart Business Exit: Getting Rewarded for Your Blood, Sweat and Tears.*

He is also a regular contributor to mainstream and online media, a popular guest on business webinars and podcasts, and a sought-after speaker on high-growth business strategies and successful business exits.

Learn more at www.grgmomentum.com.au.

CHAPTER 13

# BUILDING A WINNING TEAM

By Michael Lockwood, CFP®

I had to borrow a suit for my first job interview. I didn't have one. My friend lent me his. It didn't fit very well, and neither did the employment opportunity, to be honest. I was disappointed when I was invited to a follow-up interview.

I wasn't really interested in a career in the insurance industry at that time; the job opportunity was just one of a series of applications I had submitted, hoping something might stick somewhere. So I told the woman who contacted me that I wasn't comfortable going through another interview round because I didn't have a suit, and I couldn't bring myself to ask my buddy to lend his clearly oversized one again.

"You don't own a suit?" she said.

"No, ma'am," I told her. I explained I'd grown up with a single mom in a low-income world where no one I knew wore a suit.

"Well, come meet me in my office on Friday," she said.

That Friday she took me shopping and bought me two suits—one of which I wore to the subsequent interview and resulting job offer that opened a door to what has been my rewarding and fulfilling career in financial planning. That was thirty-seven years ago.

That kindness, prompted by her sense of belief in me, changed the course of my life, and to this day shapes some of the ways I look at business and leadership. Since that time, I have been fortunate to build a successful financial planning agency that specializes in serving people in the health care industry—it's my privilege to be able to care for people who spend their lives caring for others.

Our team of twenty at Oakwood Wealth Partners is responsible for assets totaling $1.5 billion (as of April 1, 2024), with over $260 million in active management. We have achieved this with an emphasis on building a strong team that sees the potential in every member and helping them thrive, just as that long-ago interviewer did.

# FURTHER WITH FRIENDS

Some of what I have learned about team building has come from astute business leaders like Michael E. Gerber and others, but much has also been gleaned personally from the sports world. I coached high school football for a while right out of college, but I got more deeply involved in coaching when my oldest son started playing baseball at age eight.

I didn't like what I saw at the practices: there was a lot of yelling from the coaches. I wanted to be sure that the kids were having fun rather than just being scolded, so I asked if I could help out. Over time that led to becoming the head coach for both of my sons' teams.

From the start, I told the boys I didn't care how good they were; they were going to be buddies. I wanted them to look forward to coming to practice because they were going to get to be with their friends, and we could aim to build from there. Both the players and their parents bought into this goal.

Our first season, we won one of our twenty games. Our patience in the process was tested. Four years later that team went to Cooperstown, the home of baseball, to take part in a youth tournament there. It wasn't a cheap trip—$1,500 a kid—but by that time we had built a culture that everyone (players and parents) appreciated, and we had improved together. Families had a blast— and our team finished third out of sixty-four teams. Nine of those twelve-year-old players went on to make their college baseball teams.

Of course, that approach doesn't extend fully to the business world. Having good relationships is an essential part of a healthy business, but it's not the only goal. At the end of the day, we're not there just to make friends but to make a living. I am convinced that you can make a better living when you are doing it with people who matter to you. Like with our baseball boys, you can go further with friends.

## RUNNING GOOD PLAYS

Good team building starts with the selection process. I'm not looking for a superstar player and then a bunch of backups who can help him or her be their best. I want someone with some talent, of course, but who can become part of a group that is greater than the sum of its individual parts. They also have to have a good heart with morals helping to lead their decisions.

With that in mind, I don't just go off a resume. That can only tell me so much. I want to know more about them; what drives them, what their goals are. When I finish an interview, I always ask myself if I could see having a beer with this person or going to a ball game with them? Can we do more than just function together at work?

I've learned that college athletes often make great hires. They know how to work as part of a team. They know about practicing and trying to improve. They know about taking feedback and direction. They know about getting knocked down and getting back up again. In addition to being a college athlete, they are a college scholar, with the struggles and balancing act around that.

As part of my hiring, I always ask interviewees what their life goals are, because that helps me understand how best they might fit into the team. One employee said he wanted to be making $100,000 by the time he was thirty. Another told me he wanted to work really hard for the first seven or so years and then be able to ease off a bit when he started to raise a family. Both answers were valid, and knowing what their goals were has helped me bring them into the team in a way that both we as a company and they individually are successful.

While good team building takes into account everyone's individuality, from their goals to their skills, it's not all soft and fuzzy. The best teams don't just have players who work together, they also have good plays that they run. That means accountability and systems.

We have very clear processes and expectations. We set milestones and have goals and reviews. We have two retreats a year where we work on the business (rather than in it), as Michael E. Gerber emphasizes. One gathering is to look at how well we do things internally behind the scenes and the other assesses how well we work with our clients on the front stage. We also have Christmas and other social events when we get to spend time together and with each other's families.

Goal setting for each individual and our team is a major part of our success. Failing to reach a set goal isn't treated as a problem so much as an opportunity—what do we need to learn to do better? Giving team members room to miss the mark or make a mistake is vital. If they are always worried about being called out for something that went wrong, they aren't going to stretch. They are going to be more concerned about protecting themselves and constantly underachieve to not be noticed. I want people who are willing to take risks—calculated risks, of course—because that is where the growth is.

That means I don't get mad when someone makes an honest mistake. My attitude is: it's not the end of the world; we will learn and get through this. Part of that philosophy goes back to when I was in college, working three jobs to get by and trying to get top grades. As a nineteen-year-old kid, I ended up with an ulcer. I decided that nothing was worth getting that worked up about.

# "REPOTTING" AND RESTING

If you are going to have your team members play to their strengths, you have to know what they are, of course. And that means you really need to know them as people beyond their qualifications on a piece of paper.

We use the Kolbe A™ Index and StrengthsFinder personality tests to help identify our different styles. People have different ways of looking at and approaching tasks and it is important to know what they are. For example, I am what Kolbe identifies as a "quick starter"—someone who is a bit of a risk-taker and likes to think outside the box. Those are positive qualities, but I need someone with an eye for the details to help me think things through and then execute, if it still seems like a good idea. I rate low as an "implementor": you don't want me hanging your Christmas lights, because I am likely to fall off the ladder!

Helping team members play to their strengths means being willing to make adjustments to accommodate their growth into their potential. You may have things humming along nicely the way they are right now, but if someone isn't fulfilled, eventually that is going to show. Inconvenient short-term adjustments can bring long-term benefits. You constantly have to "take the temperature."

My longtime chief of staff came to me a while ago looking for a new challenge. She was doing such a great job I didn't really want to lose her administrative skills, but I wanted to help. So, we came to an arrangement where she handled office management matters two days a week and used the rest of her time to transition to an advisor role. We call these kinds of shifts "repotting"—moving people to a new situation where they can flourish and grow and be more fruitful.

Taking care of team members isn't just about providing the tools they need to perform well while they are at work. It also means doing what you can to ensure that they have good life-work balance. If things aren't going well in their off-hours, they aren't going to be able to function at their best when they are working.

When my boys were young, I left the office early to coach their baseball games, because that was important to me. A couple of years ago, I went to one of my team members and told him he needed to start taking Fridays off. A diligent performer, he said he couldn't possibly do that.

No, I told him, he needed to do that so he could spend more time with his young family. He reluctantly agreed, and his production has actually gone up since—in part, I am sure, because of that additional quality time he is enjoying away from the office.

In my experience, when you trust people and give them freedom, they don't tend to abuse it. Even though I believed that, when the COVID-19 pandemic shut everything down, I was a little nervous about everyone working remotely full time. I needn't have worried. Not only did everything get done but our production continued to rise. I believe this all stemmed from hiring the right people, being involved in their growth, and trusting whom I hired and relied upon.

## THE "WATERFALL MENTORING" WAY

A lot of businesses talk about promoting a team culture, but they don't really have one. They may follow some kind of team-building program, but it's something they do as an exercise, not something that goes deep into their daily practices.

We emphasize team from day one. Newcomers are paired up with someone more experienced who becomes their mentor. We call it waterfall mentoring—letting what others know flow down to those coming up behind them.

This encourages an attitude of sharing and cooperation rather than competition. Some businesses have a very dog-eat-dog environment: the employees have to prove to the bosses their worth to the organizations. One member of my team who came from another insurance company recalled how she would be careful never to leave any information about a client laying around in the office because another advisor might come along and use it to try to take over the account.

That's so foreign to the way we do things. We are not that dog-eat-dog organization. Rather, we are more like a dogsled team, all pulling in the same direction. We don't just want each other to succeed, we do whatever we can to make sure that happens. And that goes beyond just mentoring and advising. One of our guys had to be out longer than expected after the birth of a child, so the advisor he was teamed with split some of his own commissions to make sure the new dad could stay home and focus on his family needs, trying to take some of the stress about money off the table.

When you have the attitude that you're all in this together, you help someone out or cover for them when they need it because you know they will do the same for you one day, when it's needed.

## SETTING THE EXAMPLE

Great teamwork isn't only important internally for an organization. It also benefits the clients. New clients are surprised when they come to their first meeting with us and learn I have assigned them two advisors to work with us.

That's because we have the clients' interest in mind, I explain. Things change—people can pass away or move on (although no one has left Oakwood in more than a decade). If that happens, we don't want our clients to have to start all over with a new advisor. We want them to be confident that there is still someone who knows them and knows their story, and can make sure their care continues seamlessly, regardless of any internal changes.

At the end of the day, you can't build a good team without being a good leader. "Do what I say, not what I do" doesn't work. People have to see you embodying the principles you espouse. You have to set the example.

My team members are diligent, but I still probably work the hardest of anyone. I'm not sitting back and coasting. I play to my strengths and give others room to play to theirs. I treat them with respect: I say please and thank you. And I have been known to have words with a client if I hear that they have been uncivil toward one of my staff. "I can't work with you if you can't treat my staff with respect," I tell them. My people know I have their back.

If ever I am tempted to forget about the importance of team or my purpose to others, I only have to glance over to my left at the wall of mentors in my office. There hang photos of six people, three of whom have passed, who either hired or coached me through my career—including the lady who bought me those first suits. Each of them looked beyond themselves and wanted me to succeed, and their example encourages me to do the same for others.

## About Mike

Mike Lockwood is an investment adviser representative with Oakwood Wealth Partners in Irvine, California. For over thirty-five years Mike has built a practice that has grown to twenty team members, with eleven advisers and nine staff members, currently overseeing over $1.5 billion in assets (as of April 1, 2024). His clientele consists of health-care professionals, governmental employees, executives, and retirees.

Mike strongly believes in working with a team approach to help his clients navigate their decisions working toward ultimate financial independence. Using a process-driven approach where we first seek to understand our values and goals, we are able to create a true partnership with our clients and their families. Mike believes it is paramount to understand the importance of these values and goals before any decisions are made.

Outstanding service and a commitment to excellence are trademarks of Mike and the Oakwood Wealth Partners team. Mike's motto is to make those around him better.

With a dual finance and marketing degree from California State University, Bakersfield, Mike has continued his education through obtaining his CERTIFIED FINANCIAL PLANNER™ practitioner in 1994. For over thirty years, he has always put the clients' best interests first and lives by Lincoln Financial Advisors' motto of Serve First, Last and Always™. He has been asked to conduct seminars on such diverse subjects as Social Security, Retirement Income Planning, Investments 101, Basic Financial Planning, and practice management.

Mike is also a published author. In December 2023 Mike released his first book, *Decision Decade*. The book addresses many of the irrevocable decisions toward retirement and the next phase of your life within the last five years before and the five years after retirement.

Mike has also been honored nationally for his commitment to the retirement planning process. He is a former board member and lifetime member of The Resource Group (TRG). TRG is an internal invitation-only, nationwide network of the top planners within Lincoln Financial Advisors. Locally, he is involved in many charities and youth sports organizations.

Outside of the office, Mike is a family man. Mike and his wife, Michelle, have been married for over thirty-two years. Their oldest son, Nick, is in his fifth year working as a financial adviser with OWP. Their youngest son, Grant, works in the financial services industry. Finally, their only daughter, Lauren, is a kindergarten teacher in Sonoma County.

You can reach Mike at

- (949) 341-4188
- Mike.Lockwood@oakwoodwp.com
- www.oakwoodwealthpartners.com

# CHAPTER 14

# FINANCIAL PSYCHOLOGISTS

By SteVan Gates

**W**hen I was growing up, I would categorize our family as being one of the affluent families from a well-to-do neighborhood. We had a nice place just a block off Weber State College campus, now a WSU. We kids went to good schools—Odgen High, Weber State, BYU, University of Utah. My parents were educated at BYU, dad a chemist, and mom an educator. We lived near some of the most successful people in the area, with PhDs, MDs, or business owners being our neighbors. And my dad was one of those very successful people. My father was the second-largest home builder in Weber County, Utah; he was the subdivision developer building over seventy-five homes a year. Had multiple companies, and he was a respected man heavily involved in his church. Just very well respected.

Life was good growing up. I played sports, we loved our family trips and a connected cousin network, my brothers and sisters were all doing well, and it was a good place and a good time to be a kid.

Then, in 1979 all of that changed for us.

Interest rates rose to 18 percent, which meant that all building and new home construction just stopped. Immediately. This was an enormous blow to the real estate industry as well as all the businesses that fed from it. Now in normal situations like this, changes in the market would be a challenge—difficult but manageable. A time to cut back, downsize, trim, and weather the storm. Except for one thing. My father—who was very good at what he did—was absolutely terrible at the planning and structure of the business part of the thing that he did so well. In his defense, "stuck to his knitting" he had a CPA on his team and other advisers but poor advice, as it turned out.

My father knew how to develop and build real estate. He was at the top of his field. Honored in the Weber Basin Home Show, but he did not know much about finance, diversification separation of entities for asset protection, the risk, or business in general. My dad did not have any contingency plan for when the market changed, rainy day fund or even a retirement plan to fall back on. Everything, all of his income and wealth, was dependent on the real estate market continuing to remain healthy. If that market was doing well, if people were still building homes and would continue to, we would be doing well because of it. If it wasn't...

The business structure my father had created involved three corporations that were making him a lot of money, but everything from those separate corporations went directly into one big corporation. So when the real estate and building industry bottomed out, all his other entities did as well, because all of them were tied to that industry. They all were pulled down together and bottomed out at the same time. Cashflow just stopped and therefore these three corporations just stopped.

As a kid, as a junior, in high school, I did not understand any of this. All I knew was that the bank was going to take the house we lived in. That we were going to have to move out of our neighborhood and go live in a rented house in a different neighborhood. That my parents would have to go to work. That I would have to go to work to help them. That things were changing and that my father had failed.

I was embarrassed. I was embarrassed at my father's failure and did not understand that 85 percent of the builders went bankrupt from 1979–1981, and I was embarrassed at where and how we now had to live. I saw the change in my parents' peace, emotions, ambitions, hope, control change, how they struggled, how the family struggled, but most importantly, I watched it break my father. I watched it change him. He never recovered emotionally.

This was the real tragedy of all of this, watching my dad who was so strong, so confident, suddenly become slow, frightened and disconnected. I sensed he was not present at times with this burden, because he had this enormous burden of debt and taxes hanging over him that he was always trying to work around.

My father was a confident, generous, loving man before 1979. But after that he never recovered mentally, emotionally, financially and he never bounced back to who he was before. I watched him drag that ball and chain of guilt and shame around for years. For decades. This embarrassment led to a loss of confidence, and I saw it affect every relationship my father had. Including the one he had with me.

When a flood, a tornado or a fire occurs, you can often recover. But although my father had to declare bankruptcy to remove the financial debt his businesses had, you cannot declare bankruptcy for federal or state taxes. This meant that there was no real *moving on* from this part because this huge tax debt had to be paid. So my father would work odd jobs for years to save money, and when he had over $36,000 saved up, the IRS would take it right out of his account. It was a reminder, year after year to him, of what a business failure he had become.

The IRS had garnished his wages and took money from his account, for over twenty years, until my father was seventy-seven years old when they offered him a compromise deal.

This event in my family's life was the genesis of my interest in economics and financial planning, because I saw a bad plan, ruin a good man and many careers of those is associated industries. It was a tsunami and cascade of destruction, and I saw how emotional money was tied to all of us. So I began to research and plan my own. I did a research paper at WSU called "Common-Cents" with reference to money, dollars and Cents. Additionally, business management financial planning structures could not only help people like my father but would also be safe for myself for when changes occurred out of my control, as they did to my family.

Later on I discovered Michael Gerber, who was at the time the Michael Jordan of business owners, where he teaches people how to have a business, not just have a job. Gerber's superpower was teaching entrepreneurs the oxygen of repeatable, sustainable, scalable business, it's called processes and systemization. In fact, the term, "If it's a problem, make it a process" resonated with me. Also, you have to work *on* your business, not just *in* your business as assume it all works out. Other coaches and consultants kept pointing to Gerber's core and foundational nature of business processes and systemization before you can take flight and get to your intended destinations.

Through his books I learned that as a business owner I would first need to wear many hats, because I didn't have the revenue to hire ten people right off the bat. But what I learned from *The E-Myth* was about the systems, processes, and teams. I saw right away the wisdom and the intelligence behind these processes, these systematic things. But also the emotional connection to your profession, your business and your clients/customers. I saw that I could be the very best version of myself, because I could have these skilled systems and processes in place. So I began to plan to work *on* my business before I started working *in* it.

I created the plan for my practice, which was twenty years ago, and I jumped in and, as an independent financial fiduciary, sought to understand where my clients were in their planning continuum and where they wanted to go, which I call the ideal future. Then, with the savvy use of modeling scenarios and best-in-class planning strategies, Gates Planning and Consulting developed. That later evolved into a merger and acquisition of Financial Strategies Institute/Securities America Inc./OSIAC, and recently I had my business valued at just north of seven million dollars.

Over the years with my business, it's been so gratifying seeing people with a little bit of money saved grow their wealth, listen to and execute best-in-class planning strategies, and then with financial independence make the transition to financial independence and wealth distribution strategies. How does my company do that? Because we do not bank our plans on hope. Our plans are based on the best practices in the industry, thought leaders and some of the best of the best. I've had the privilege to serve on multiple advisory boards and advisors' councils. Now in the *top* 3 percent of my peers across the country. We are recession resistance. And we do not rely on external forces for success or worry about them breaking us in serving our clients.

Because negative external forces will happen. They did for my dad, but we have the ability to give our clients a plan that will deal with the risks of volatility, taxes, longevity and other uncontrolled macroeconomics. We have a plan that gives them clarity, simplicity, peace of mind, and confidence. They want a confident future.

But one of the biggest reasons we have become so successful is through team of other complementary specialists, such as for taxes, legal documents, or an insurance specialist—I call it a "virtual family office" format that we have built. And this really accelerated from COVID. As many other silver linings from COVID, virtual work, Zoom, DocuSign, telehealth accelerated technology was institutionalized.

Many interesting advances came after the pandemic, from the discovery of vaccines and other medical advances, but in business there were some incredible tools we began to use. And those tools allow us to grow and serve clients not just limited to our region, then coupled with the very best talent available and be virtual.

Zoom calling is now mainstream, and with a five-minute notice I can be videoconferencing with anyone from around the world. DocuSign is amazing—how crazy is that? We do not go to the bank, we do not have to go to the title company, and we do not have to go somebody's office to sign anything—we can just do it all virtually.

Telehealth was a big advancement, and I saw that we could take this concept and develop our own version. The doctors in the hospital are smart, but not as smart as when they connect to other doctors, labs, X-rays, EKGs, CT scans, and outcomes around the world using artificial intelligence (AI), which are doing research and breakthroughs in other areas. And I can now do the same thing in my industry.

If there is a client of mine who is feeling economic pain or a financial fever, that can be treated quickly. They can call me, we can jump on Zoom, I can share the screen, and we can analyze the client's financial health. And I can tap into experts and thought leaders that I am partnered with all around the world. Now, with the explosion of AI, which taps into a human intelligence team from all around the world.

I have discovered that AI may not put me out of business, as it will for some people and industries, but my competitors that are savvier at using AI may take greater market share.

Together we look at the financial picture using the best modeling and diagnostics software and the plan together. Then we ask questions. "What if we did this?" or, "What if this bad thing happens—how should we react?" We go through these multiple models together. Try on "What if this?" What if that?" and the quantifiable difference. It's huge! That's what we do in the financial planning and wealth management world. We work with and can tie in the best of the best, creating my virtual family office networks of specialists around the world.

I have access to the *top of the top* financial fiduciaries across the country to vet out certain things that are sustainable, that work, and that we're not chasing the shiny things of the world or chasing the next fad darling, but solid metrics, solid growth, time tested. My clients are not expecting to double their money in three years, because we are dealing with forces that are out of our control. We use things that really work and that clients can understand. And *not* those things that work really well for a period of time until they don't work.

With my clients, the goal is often to understand where they are, where they want to go and by when and their goals and objective.

And their desired lifestyle. It's all about life style, income certainty of that life style and achieving that with certainty, not hope. Hope is not a plan. Then making mid-course corrections yearly as needed and providing that clarity and confidence. We do not focus on why their accounts are way up, nor do we focus on why accounts may be down, but they are *on track* for the success of their goals! And so I set expectations that have a solid history behind them. Because I've learned that with risk there's also variables out of our control. And some of these risky ventures, or the hot tip from a neighbor or family member. If the clients want to be involved with it, that are really risky, then I say, "Hey, let's limit maybe 5–10 percent max. But if you want to do it, I will let you know what there is out there and either do it on your own, or I will send you somewhere else. Or perhaps they are just not a fit for me or my team.

If people have peace of mind and clarity on their finances, income, lifestyle, and estate objectives, then we've done our job. You can have somebody that has ten million or a hundred million dollars, and they may not have total clarity. The amount does not give it to you because it could evaporate quickly. You could be one volatile situation with the risk and inadvertently following the path my father did.

The goal is to have a plan that works over the long term, whether markets are good, or markets are bad, whether economics are good or economics are bad. "Retirees that have these things—that have stability, certainty to their income and lifestyle—live longer."

There have been studies in behavioral economics that show that "when your financial stress goes up, your emotional competence goes down, and your irrational decision-making behavior goes up, and your physical and financial health goes down. It's called *misery* :/ But when your financial stress goes down, your emotional competence goes up, your irrational decision-making behavior goes down, and your physical and financial health goes up," called *wisdom*! Its also called "the health and wealth connection." So that is really what we really do, we are financial psychologists, and we do not only manage money; we have to manage people's expectations and fears and worries. Which leads them to be healthier and happier and lead fulfilling lives. So, you can have all the money in the world but if you are not healthy because you were in have too much stress, it does not matter how much money you have.

And that is what we do and what I will continue to do. And it is because of Michael Gerber influence in the underlying business structure and processes in serving our valued clientele and managing my very successful practice.

And it is to help people and families never to go through what my father went through.

## About SteVan

For over thirty years SteVan H. Gates has offered strategies in investment management, financial independence, retirement transitions, social security, business succession, income tax reduction strategies, life insurance, estate planning, and the financial and emotional issues involved in wealth transition. He's engaged in a three-appointment step-by-step process to assist in making smart decisions, protecting wealth, keeping more of what they make, taking care of heirs and making a difference with his specialization and his amazing, experienced *team* behind him. His clients have appreciated the clarity, simplicity, and confidence in their financial future. SteVan's modeling has created dynamic strategies always evolving to try on the "what if" scenarios tailored for each client's goals and objectives. He is always providing financial and educational workshops year after year to inform and empower clients. SteVan's clients have become dear friends, trusted relationships, and advocates.

Honors, Education, and Experience:

- Securities America Advisory Council Member 2020 (15 Council Members of 2,800-plus Advisors)
- Published in Advisors Magazine Safety First: Tackle the Threats to Your Nest Eggs
- Botsford Elite Advisor Alumni 2018
- Chair of the Prestigious Allegis Advisor Group Advisory Board 2015 and 2016
- With Allegis Investment Advisors
- Selected to the Elite Lincoln Financial Advisors/Sagemark Consulting Private Wealth Service Group
- A Sagemark Private Wealth Svcs. 2007, 2008, 2009, 2010, and 2013
- Over thirty years' experience in the financial services and wealth-planning disciplines
- Nationally recognized speaker for Retirement Income and Wealth Protection and Investment Strategies

- Director of Professional Development 1997–2001 Lincoln Financial Advisors, Salt Lake City, Utah
- Manager of the Year in 2000
- CRPC®—Chartered Retirement Planning Counselor from the College for Financial Planning
- CFP®—Student @ Bryn Mawr College Pennsylvania, College for Financial Planning
- BFA®—Behavioral Financial Advisor candidate
- Alumnus of Economics at the University of Utah and Communications at Weber State University
- Family: SteVan and his wife, Jolene, of thirty-nine years live in Farmington, Utah. They have four fantastic children: David, Nathan, Michael, and Lexie. SteVan enjoys travel, charitable interests, reading, working in his yard, being a PARC Board Member, golfing, skiing, and hiking the backcountry.
- SteVan H. Gates, CRPC, is a registered representative with Securities America Inc. Member FINRA & SIPC. Advisory services offered through Securities America Advisors Inc. Financial Strategies Institute and Securities America are not affiliated.

www.ingramcontent.com/pod-product-compliance
Lightning Source LLC
Chambersburg PA
CBHW070700190326
41458CB00046B/6803/J